REINVENT YOUR REALITY

*A Positively Practical Guide to
Revitalize Your Life & Work*

SALLY ANNE CARROLL

Copyright © 2022 by Sally Anne Carroll

All rights reserved. No part of this publication may be reproduced, distributed or transmitted in any form or by any means, including photocopying, recording, or other electronic or mechanical methods, without the prior written permission of the publisher, except in the case of brief quotations embodied in critical reviews and certain other noncommercial uses permitted by copyright law. For permission requests, contact the author at:

Sally Anne Carroll / Artisan Communications
www.sallyannecarroll.com

Reinvent Your Reality / Sally Anne Carroll. — 1st ed.

Paperback ISBN: 979-8-9850671-2-5
Hardcover ISBN: 979-8-9850671-3-2

DEDICATION

To your next chapter, and everything that becomes possible on the journey from here to there.

CONTENTS

INTRODUCTION		7
CHAPTER ONE	*MAYBE THIS SOUNDS FAMILIAR...*	13
CHAPTER TWO	*PREPARING FOR THE JOURNEY*	27
CHAPTER THREE	*RECONNECT*	41
CHAPTER FOUR	*REIMAGINE*	59
CHAPTER FIVE	*REVITALIZE*	79
CHAPTER SIX	*REDESIGN*	103
CHAPTER SEVEN	*REALIGN*	119
CHAPTER EIGHT	*RESTRUCTURE*	143
CHAPTER NINE	*WHAT'S POSSIBLE NOW*	165
REFERENCES AND FURTHER READING		177
GRATITUDE		181
ABOUT THE AUTHOR		183

INTRODUCTION

As I stood barefoot in the snow watching my home in flames, the resistance fell away. I'd been clinging to a job and a lifestyle that was no longer working, and I knew it.

There was no more hiding. This was the final straw in a series of changes that life had thrown at me. The message was clear: It was time to take back control and create the changes I craved. There was (literally) nothing left of the life that I had built, except for my job that, while it had once felt like a great fit, was now stressing me out and keeping me stuck. Sitting in the fire of reinvention in all areas of my life at once, I realized I'd been clinging to any pieces that felt safe, even though I knew that there was more and better out there for me. The time had come to take back power and start making choices instead of reacting to the choices that were being made for me.

This book is one I wish I had when I was deciding what was next for me, personally and professionally. I sensed that I had been holding myself back, keeping myself safe, and shrinking my life for too long, but I didn't know how to solve the problem. On that day, I decided to find out and intended to grow myself through the process.

You don't have to wait for a crisis to throw you into reinvention. In most cases, reinvention comes in the shape of a career pivot or plateau, a geographic move, starting a new business, a wellness journey, or totally redesigning your lifestyle. I opted to tackle all of these areas at once, but I don't necessarily recommend this route. You may instead want to make the changes you most desire step by step and allow your reinvention to evolve and open new doors as you close the old ones—one by one.

Whichever route you choose, I want to make it easier for you.

ARE YOU READY TO REINVENT YOUR REALITY?

I have coached many clients standing at the edge of reinventing their careers and lifestyles. This book is the foundation of what I know to be true about the process and the internal and external growth required to make significant changes at work and at home. Over time, I have identified six distinct phases that are essential to successfully reinventing any area of your life.

I blend life coaching and career coaching in my work intentionally because we do not live separate "personal lives" and "professional lives." We live *one life*, one that requires us to show up in many areas (not just those two). Integrating the pieces effectively and authentically takes a unique combination of practice, art, and science. This balance creates sustainable success to live your best life.

This road may not always be easy, but it is not complicated, and it is attainable. It will challenge you and grow you—and your results will always be worth the investment. This book is in your hands because I want you to know that you can have what you want without having to figure it out all on your own. If your inner dialogue sounds anything like this, then you're in the right place:

I know I have to leave this soul-sucking job, but hey, I'm lucky to have it. I'll manage. And besides, what would I do anyway?

I've always dreamed of working for myself, but I never seem to have enough courage to launch that dream.

I would love to work from home and be in complete control of my schedule; it must be great to take a yoga class in the middle of the day (it is, by the way). I don't think I could ever do that.

I wish I had [insert whomever you secretly stalk online here] life. She's always going places and having fun adventures, and she and her partner seem so in love.

I feel like there's more to life. I just know that I am meant to make a bigger contribution—but how do I even figure out what that is and where to start?

This economy is the worst possible time to be looking for a new job, moving to a new city, or upending the status quo. But now I have no choice.

You do have a choice! You can think differently about what's possible for you. You can reimagine, realign, and restructure, inviting in more of what you truly want, what energizes you, and what pulls you forward.

If it's a new career you want, you can have that. If you want to work from home, there's never been a better time. You can have a better work-life balance, a higher income, more purpose in your days, get that dream project off the ground, spend more time traveling, or just enjoying the success you're building. All of this is possible.

HOW TO GET THE MOST OUT OF THIS BOOK

Let this book guide and coach you. Use a handwritten journal or create a folder on your desktop and do all of the exercises. Give each one time and space, and carefully digest each section. You may want to revisit sections of this book as you progress toward your new reality; I encourage you to work through these steps the first time in the order they are presented. After much experience and experimentation in my own life and in coaching my clients through this process, I have found this order to be the most effective.

You can download exercise worksheets at www.wholelifestrategies.com/ryrworkbook or scan the QR code on page 176.

You may find that you come back to this book again and again. I want it to be an inspiring and continual companion as you shed old stories, imagine new possibilities, and get busy with creating your new reality.

The desire to reinvent even the smallest piece of your lifestyle or your workday can be transformative. Imagine feeling clear about who you are and what matters most to you in this next chapter. Imagine uncovering the new story for what is possible for you. Imagine that you have let go of the self-doubt and the stuckness, and have a vision for what's next. Imagine that you are confident in your plan of action.

On my journey of reinventing nearly everything in my life, I've learned that we are never truly done. The process is a journey;

there is no destination. You will come back to what you learn in this book, again and again, evolving with each season in your life.

I guarantee that you will have moments of doubt and moments when clarity and confidence suddenly feel out of reach. That's all part of stepping into the unknown and creating something new. This book offers the process for walking through those mini re-inventions with grit, grace, and a deep sense of who you are and what matters most to you.

My goal is to inspire and encourage you. So, create space to exhale, breathe deeply, and just be you. If you're not sure who you are right now, relax; this is your chance to find out. I provide a clear path to follow and practical tools to help you navigate effectively through change.

Here is your opportunity to create what's next for you holistically and expansively. It also welcomes and offers tools for working through fear, uncertainty, and doubt (we're not getting rid of our brains—we will learn to work with them).

If we were working one-on-one together, we would begin with this framework, and here's what I would tell you:

There has never been a better time to step back and take a clear-eyed, honest look at what you really, really want—and how to get there—than in this moment when you're being called to make changes. Of course, there's work involved, but I also know that as soon as you start taking the steps to launch yourself into that reinvention, life will meet you there.

It is possible. Let this book show you where to begin and give you the support you need to keep going.

CHAPTER ONE
MAYBE THIS SOUNDS FAMILIAR...

Everything in my body was telling me that this is no way to live.

But I was only half-listening.

I worked 50+ hours a week in a fast-growing consulting firm. My commute was 90 minutes each way and even longer during New England's snowy winters. I was great at my job; it offered me continual new challenges and opportunities to develop new skills, and it stretched me professionally. I was taking on new roles and growing a department. The firm's leadership rewarded me with salary increases, bonuses, high-impact projects, and educational and ownership opportunities with a clear path to leadership. I was, by all accounts, a rising star with a promising future. On paper, it all made perfect sense.

I was also bored with the content of the work, exhausted, miserable, and sure that I was heading in the wrong direction. At the start, I'd suspected that the company and role weren't the right cultural fit, and day by day, it was becoming increasingly clear—it was certainly not a lifestyle fit. I'd become skilled at climbing what intuitively felt like the wrong ladder, and despite knowing it was time to jump off, I wasn't moving.

At the time, I was also developing a side hustle as an editorial and marketing consultant with my eye on making my corporate escape. Juggling two demanding work priorities, I was arriving home in time to eat, sleep, wake up, and repeat. I began living for weekends when my then-partner (who had a similar routine) and I would finally relax, hit Home Depot, and work on settling into our new home.

As a lifelong writer, I had also been nurturing a couple of creative projects and was offered a four-week writing retreat in the woods of Minnesota to focus on my work. Believing that I could not leave my life and my job for a month, I negotiated for two (instead of four) glorious, quiet, writing-filled weeks. When I left my cabin on the lake, I arrived home feeling grateful for the experience and everything in my life. Most critically, the new level of clarity that I needed to make a radical change in my professional life and fast.

Sometimes, life pushes you. Before I had the chance to put change in motion, a string of events occurred that would change many parts of my life and not in the ways I intended. Within months, my family had lost someone dear to cancer, and my marriage seemed to be abruptly and unexpectedly careening to an end. Five months later, I was involved in a car accident that kept me from work for three months. I made good use of that time to immerse myself in figuring out what was next. I was invited back to the writing retreat that summer and spent the time walking in nature and writing. When I returned, another unexpected development greeted me: A nonprofit organization that I knew and loved invited me to apply for a position.

Accepting that job was the easiest work-related decision I had made in a long time, even though it came with a few significant tradeoffs. Unlike my last role that felt like a treadmill, this one was fun, highly creative, and collaborative. It came with the things I craved that play right to my strengths: more autonomy and a flexible work schedule. It also came with a heavy workload, a small staff, never-ending deadlines, and eventually, a fair amount of stress. For a while, I didn't care. I loved it. But it wasn't long before I found myself sitting for hours on end at my computer, working well after 7 p.m., and losing what little resources we had to numerous budget cuts.

To ensure that I was fueled for the changes and challenges I was facing, I devoted my personal time in a new way to self-renewal, reading, and personal growth. I took long walks in the woods near my home and had even longer conversations with friends and family. I immersed myself in learning, growing, exploring, trying new things, and making new personal connections. It was an incredibly creative, nourishing, and deeply challenging time, and my life got even more interesting after I chose to enlist coaching support.

At the start of our relationship, one of my coaches asked me what I really wanted for myself. I had absolutely no idea how to answer her question. No one had ever asked me that before, and it had been a long time since I had seriously asked myself. I'd spent my entire adult life in a partnership and my professional life doing what I thought was expected of me, so the question was always more about "what's best for us."

Together, we made a list as I lounged in the hammock under the trees in my front yard. I started reimagining the possibilities (*hmmm, why couldn't I do that?*) and designing ways to make these things happen, testing this, and trying that. I was on my way to discovering what I wanted to build for myself. And then life stepped in, throwing me another curveball.

My home—my sanctuary during all the chaos and which I had alternated between renovating and leaving behind—went up in flames one December night. There's nothing like losing everything you've worked for to give you a new perspective on what matters and what's next. Witnessing the home I'd worked for, the place I felt most safe, burning was one of the most challenging things I have had to experience. I now had a clean slate, whether I wanted one or not. That can make reinventing easier, but it can also make it so much harder.

After a few months of healing and deliberation, I felt the nudge turn to a push. I heeded the call and chose to go all-in. Starting with a week-long mindfulness retreat to clear my head, I started the process of selling my property, quitting my job, and making plans to move across the country. I decided to give myself a couple of months to regroup, using the relationships I'd made through my side hustle to work part-time and meet my longtime dream of being self-employed. I drove from coast to coast, leaning on friends and family to keep me in momentum, and plunged myself headlong into getting to know a new city—and a whole new side of myself.

When I reflect on this time, in some ways, I can hardly recognize the past me, although I'm grateful for the difficult choices that she made. My coast-to-coast adventure took me to Portland, Oregon, where I still live. I have split my time between here and New Zealand, where my husband was born and raised, for many years. I took my side hustle work full-time and ran a successful location-independent consulting practice for several years. As part of my desire to keep learning, I trained as a professional coach and started a second business, one that has pulled all of the pieces of my life together in a new way.

I also see how easy it would have been to stay comfortable and not make decisions that I knew I had to make for so long even when life started trying to make some of them for me. Instead, I started asking the tough questions, imagining new possibilities, and designing my life around what matters to me and what naturally gives me energy. I haven't stopped doing that. For the most part, I live the life born from that initial active exploration of my questions and that's still evolving with the continual asking: *What's next? What do I want to create now? What do I really, really want (and need)? What's possible now? What will that require of me?*

Those are still some of the most pertinent and thought-provoking questions I ask myself and every one of my clients. Asking and answering those questions repeatedly for our lifetime, as we become the 2.0, 3.0, and 4.0 versions of ourselves.

Reinventing your career and your lifestyle is thrilling, creative, life-affirming, and terrifying. It asks you to step up into growth and choice, and that's a powerful business. I've spent so much time, energy, and money learning how to do it well that I consider it my life's work.

This book has been brewing from the beginning. It's the companion and inspiration I wanted but couldn't find because I was writing it through my experiences. I sincerely hope that it paves the way for making the minor tweaks and big shifts that will give you a life and a career you love—and the tools to allow yourself to reinvent and evolve as you grow.

It is what you deserve. You absolutely can create it, even if, especially if, it looks nothing like anything that has come before.

IT STARTS WITH A CHOICE

Before we get started, there is one foundational belief that is critical to the process of reinvention, and that is this: You always have choices.

Often, we don't make changes that we crave because a part of us believes that we don't have a choice. We are all capable of spinning awe-inspiring stories around this simple issue of thinking and decision-making. Our brains can be masters at keeping us safe, and sometimes "safe" can mean stuck.

I can speak to this myself. When I was accepting unfulfilling jobs after graduating from university, that was less about the recession I'd graduated into and more about the expectation that I would find work connected to my degree and work my way up the ladder. I believed that until I found the right role, I had to find a paycheck while I did what I loved on the side. I worked a lot, hustled, and followed the rules as I knew them.

It did not occur to me at the time that I had many other choices, rules, and models available to me that may have been more appropriate for me to follow. It may sound crazy now to think that I hadn't really thought to look outside the box that I knew, but in coaching, I find that many of my clients have had this experience, too. I'm sure it's true of many more people on this planet than I will ever meet. We're hardwired as humans to stay safe and comfortable, and there's nothing wrong, really, with safe and comfortable. But for many of us, that is not the path to unlocking our potential or building lives that sustain us and fulfill us for the long term.

One of the most profound lessons I have learned in my own life and career is that I am always making a choice about my experience. We all are. Even when circumstances feel like they will overwhelm us, even when all of the choices we can think of seem less than desirable, we *always* have choices. There are many different ways to resolve an issue, but most of the time, we're focused on the one or two ways that we know best, the ones we've already tried, the ones that have gotten us here.

Our human brains are designed to scan our environment, predict events based on past experience, and assess our results according to what happens. When we are aware of this, we can start to create small openings between a situation and our response so that we can see other options and allow our brains the opportunity to predict from new experiences.

As you begin your own journey to reinvention, I want you to hold on to this truth. There are always ways to create more of what you want or need. There are plenty of paths to fulfillment and sustainable success. There are always choices that will allow you to experience more of what matters to you in your daily life, even when you can't see them clearly. By the end of this book, you'll be a lot better at finding them, testing them, and exploring new options for what's possible for you.

INTRODUCING...
THE SIX STAGES OF REINVENTION

I define reinvention as creating a new normal in your life, your career, your contribution to the world, or (often) all three because they're all interconnected. Although reinvention sounds like a big undertaking—and it is consequential in ways that change everything—we will all experience it at some point. We will all grow and change in ways large and small. We will shed previous versions of ourselves. We will experience life transitions, and we will likely change job roles or professions.

The pace of change in our world is increasing, so it's imperative that we learn how to make change work for us. Those who successfully navigate these large and small reinventions have things in common, such as a willingness to ask themselves powerful questions, assess their current reality, dream bigger than they've been dreaming, clear the murky waters of possibility, and develop a solid underpinning that allows them to be brave, experiment, and create something new.

In my experience, no matter what we're reinventing, there are six distinct stages we experience. We need to give each stage its due so that we can clearly and confidently get where it is we want to go. My six-stage framework for coaching personal and professional reinvention—the inspiration for and the subject matter of the remainder of this book—breaks it down as follows.

RECONNECT

When attempting to reinvent any area of your life or all of it, it's important to understand the ground where you currently stand. You can't know where you are headed until you know where you are. Reconnecting isn't just about your current situation; it's also a deep dive into what makes you uniquely you and how you are showing up right now in your life and career. In this stage, you take a clear-eyed look at your reality as it stands right now—what is working and not working. How is your quality of life on an objective scale? Where are your priorities, and how are they reflected in your day to day? You'll also reconnect to your core values, needs, and natural strengths, as well as your skillset and interests. Mindset, your "inner game," is also a critical part of reconnection, so you'll examine your beliefs and how they may be helping or hindering your happiness.

REIMAGINE

Once you've spent time learning more about who you are and examining the current circumstances of your personal and professional life, you're rooted enough to reimagine what's possible for your life. You'll begin with the 30,0000-foot view so that you can think expansively about what it is you truly want in all areas of your life and engage the parts of your brain that enhance strategic thinking and natural motivation. In this stage, you will also explore a concept I call "freedom to and freedom from" to broaden your thinking around what you most want to create and identify factors that contribute to your definitions of meaning and purpose. Imagine your new future, one that stretches your ideas of what you can have. The fun work is pulling this all together in a vision that pulls you forward.

REVITALIZE

Reinvention is a journey, and as with any travel, it pays to be well prepared. The Revitalize stage is focused on clearing the space needed to do any inner and outer work required to put your vision into an actionable plan. This space is physical, emotional, mental, and spiritual, and your goal is to identify and manage obstacles that could prevent you from showing up as your most powerful, clear, and confident self. It's also about giving yourself what you need to manage your energy along the way. You'll continue to upgrade your mindset and identity beliefs, and you'll also integrate meaningful, evidence-based energy management and self-care practices that will nourish you and establish a foundation for creating sustainable success.

REDESIGN

Now, it's time to get down to tangible plans and goals and activate your vision. While many people make the mistake of trying to begin here, when you arrive at this stage fully prepared, you'll have much more clarity and confidence than if you had tried to jump into planning from the start. You will identify a clear starting point to focus on, curate your life so that you can test and try out your ideas, set goals, and create a personal strategic plan that identifies your gaps and how to fill them. You'll identify what you need to learn (and unlearn), use your self-awareness and design thinking principles to map out a direction, identify meaningful experiments, and break them down into doable actions.

REALIGN

Realigning is all about truth-testing your emerging plans against real life; it's your reality check. As you experiment with putting your plans into action, you'll find the natural places to realign your vision with what you're discovering and what might keep you from moving forward with your plans—or even expanding them. Engineering change is 80% about how you're showing up, and we will explore how you can continue to inspire and empower yourself to create what's next for you. You'll discover practical tools for slaying challenges, staying motivated, and handling the typical obstacles that come with uncertainty and change (hello, fear, self-doubt, limiting beliefs!).

RESTRUCTURE

The final stage is where you walk into your bigger vision by restructuring your life around your plan and making decisions. While you will continue to experiment and investigate, things start to feel more settled. You'll also learn to build the scaffolding you need to support your new life and work. You'll build evidence for your dreams, develop inspired next steps, and find affirming ways to befriend resistance and fear to move you forward.

In this stage, you will embody your reinvention in a way that builds your capacity for creating at new and higher levels for your life. It may seem like this is the end of the road—you might have already made big changes or identified a new career—but we are never really done. When you reach where you were going, you'll then create what's next from a different vantage point—and in fact, a different self—than where you began. In other words, these are skills and ways of being that you can customize and call on for life.

REINVENTION REMINDERS

- You always have choices. If you've felt like you need to make some changes in your lifestyle, work style, or both, you're probably right. Knowing that you always have a choice can free you up to see what's possible for you.

- Reinvention is a process. You are not expected to know what's next for you until you've followed that process. Or, as Dr. Martin Luther King, Jr. said, "You don't need to see the whole staircase, you just have to know the next step."

- The Six Stages of Reinvention may overlap, and you may go through a reinvention cycle more than once. In every case, you want to begin with the important foundational work that is key to your success in the later stages of identifying and planning your next moves.

REINVENTION CYCLE
for sustainable success

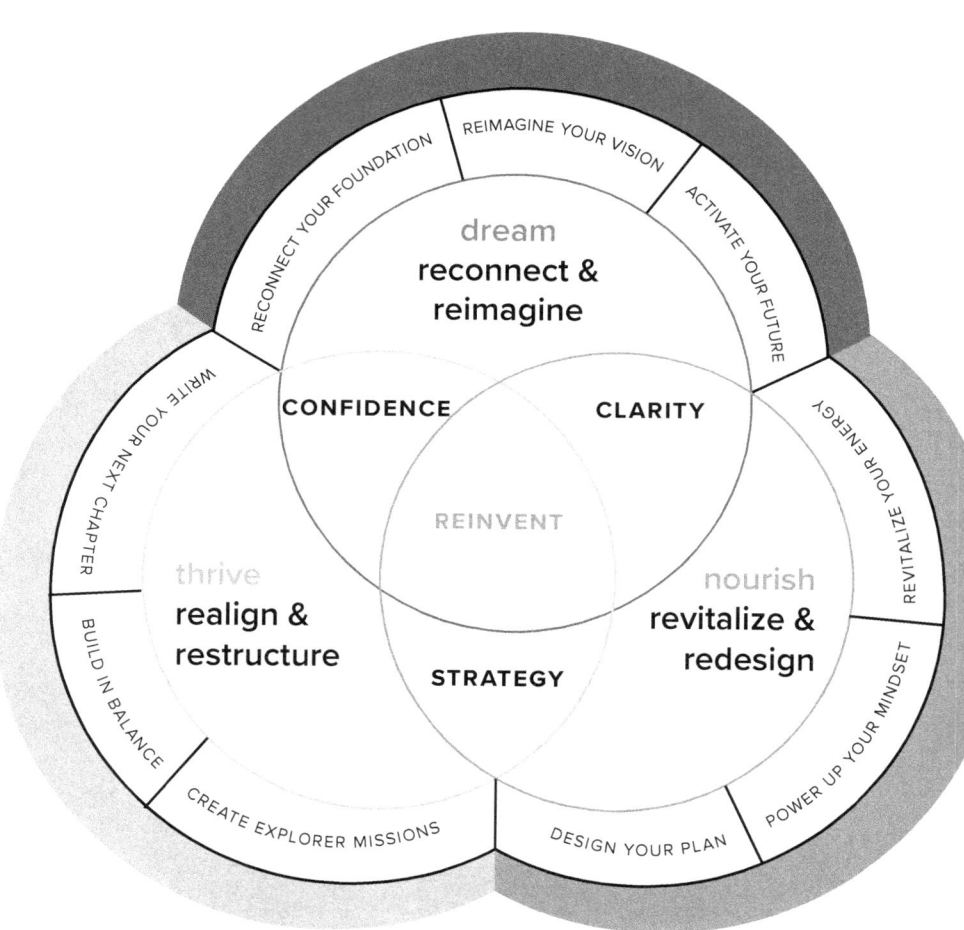

dream **reconnect & reimagine**

RECONNECT YOUR FOUNDATION
Assess your strengths, values, priorities, and needs for a solid foundation.

REIMAGINE YOUR VISION
Expand your view of what's possible. What do you really want?

ACTIVATE YOUR FUTURE
Find your most impactful starting point and commit.

---

nourish **revitalize & redesign**

REVITALIZE YOUR ENERGY
Uplevel your self-care to make room for reinvention.

POWER UP YOUR MINDSET
Cultivate thinking and evidence to support your goals.

DESIGN YOUR PLAN
Create the strategic roadmap from here to there.

---

thrive **realign & restructure**

CREATE EXPLORER MISSIONS
Explore your options. Experiment. Do your research.

BUILD IN BALANCE
Realign your plan with what you've learned and make it sustainable.

WRITE YOUR NEXT CHAPTER
Celebrate your accomplishments and prepare your next steps.

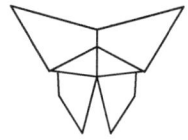

YOUR NEXT STEP

Let's take a moment to set the stage for the exploration you're about to go on.

- Decide where you will record your discoveries and reflections while you're reading this book.

- Set aside committed time to do the exercises, practices, and experiments that you'll read as you go forward. Put that time on your calendar now.

In the next chapter, we will lay the groundwork, beginning with setting intentions and exploring common myths about the journey that you're about to go on.

CHAPTER TWO
PREPARING FOR THE JOURNEY

As a coach, I advocate for thinking bigger in our lives; this book is also designed with real-life sustainability in mind. Practical changes that stick, the foundation for real-life reinventions, happen step by step. By the end of this book, what I want for you is to:

- Feel empowered to choose—and start creating—what you really want.

- Reconnect to yourself and feel inspired to unleash your reinvention energy.

- Create a solid vision for your reinvention that reflects your values and priorities.

- Start with your most burning desire or place of biggest impact and make real progress.

- Mold this step-by-step process into personal practices that you can use to kick-start change wherever you need it.

WHAT TO EXPECT ALONG THE WAY

No matter how it happens or how wanted or unwanted, expected or unexpected, creating big change will inevitably bring up your drama, your perceived limitations, your old arguments, and even a few habits you thought you'd left behind. You can count on this. Redesigning and realigning will require that you learn to navigate all of that in a way that allows you to grow.

Please take heart that this is all part of the process. It does not need to keep you spinning your wheels or getting stuck. By learning to be present for all of it, you can learn to navigate effectively, and you will come out the other side with tools, strategies, and ways of being that will help you continue to navigate small and large changes throughout your life. Here are five of my favorite strategies for noticing when this is happening and staying in (or returning to) your own momentum.

EMBRACE YOUR EDGES

When you're at the edge of what is comfortable and familiar, mastery can feel like a faraway destination. You will not be perfect at what you are just learning to do. Everyone experiences learning curves; it takes time to move from uncertainty to a place of calm confidence. I first learned the concept of stretching yourself right to your edges so that your edges can soften and expand as a 20-year-old yoga student. It translates beautifully to reinventions of all kinds. Standing right at the edge of what is comfortable for you and allowing your comfort zone to gradually expand with practice always works better than avoiding your edges altogether or pushing yourself too far, too fast.

What if... you jumped in with both feet to being consciously incompetent at first and practicing your way to how and where you want to be?

DON'T ARGUE WITH RESISTANCE

When you're at your edges, it's not unusual to suddenly love the status quo (you know, those same things you have been yearning and attempting to change). That's normal. I know from experience that fighting our natural resistance to change is not only futile, but it will also often set you back. So, if you don't want to take the next step right this minute, or you want to go running back to the old you for a day or two, just notice that. You can be curious about it instead of making yourself wrong for feeling that way. Be aware of what you're really needing at this time and let go of any self-judgment. More often than not, when you're not fighting against it, resistance will subside on its own and offer important information that will help you move back into action.

What if... you were simply present for what you're feeling right now?

DROP YOUR DRAMA

We all expect a bit of mind drama to come up when tumultuous changes throw us out of our comfort zone, and that drama can come with even the smallest of changes. For example, a few years ago, my body was navigating major hormonal shifts, and my doctor suggested that letting myself sleep in was one of the best things I could do for my health at that time. I did not want to listen. Instead, the self-created drama went like this: *I can't sleep late. I have things to do. Productive people get up early. I have a routine. I already get plenty of sleep.* She calmly refuted my arguments: *You create your own schedule. You can always keep one day a week for early appointments. Sleep is productive. Who says you have to be up so early?* Eventually, I dropped my drama for facts. My body needed more sleep than it had before, and I am fortunate that I can adjust to a more flexible schedule if needed. Not surprisingly, when I stopped fighting for my limitations and focused on facts, I was able to more easily get the results I wanted. Whether it's your schedule or your self-care, finances, relationship, or career, if the story you're telling can be refuted, it's more likely drama than fact.

What if... you dropped the drama and stuck to the facts?

TAKE A TIMEOUT

While many of us do try, you cannot keep up the momentum, build capacity for change, or do your best creative thinking when you are tired, worn out, overwhelmed, or over-scheduled. As you engage with the ideas in this book, taking time to rest and to be is invaluable. For me, this has taken the form of a short morning meditation, a tech-free Sunday, or limiting the endless barrage of news or social obligations. My clients take time out in the form of a daily walk on a nearby beach, ten minutes of silence at the start and the end of the day, twice-weekly workout dates with a friend, or a whole weekend away. Once a week, once a day—ten minutes or two hours—try starting small and making this gift to yourself super easy to implement. Even five minutes can shift your busy pattern and create new habits that will enhance your resilience. Carving out space for a non-negotiable timeout can be challenging, but it is also worth the effort and the discomfort it takes to create these essential bits of space in and around your life.

What if... you invested some quiet time in yourself?

STEP FULLY INTO THE CHANGE YOU ARE SEEKING

Commitment is the first step of making anything happen. Your decisions are powerful. Whether you've agreed to entertain a new possibility, embraced a new way of being, or decided on a new course of action, you want to do what you know is needed to step fully into your new reality. You will never know how it works out until you do.

A FEW THINGS TO UNDERSTAND ABOUT REINVENTION

As a world right now, we are in transition. Global change is accelerating, whether we like it or not, and for many of us, this change has had significant impacts on our lives and/or careers. I work every day with professionals who are navigating unexpected job loss, switching careers, stepping up as leaders, building businesses; they're also moving house, moving in or out of relationships, trying to make sense of loss, change, and disruptions to their daily lives. And that was before a global pandemic.

YOU ALREADY KNOW HOW TO DO THIS

As much as modern life might shake our foundations, we are all equipped for this journey. Life itself is all about change and transition. As humans, we are always growing, being stretched, experiencing something for the first time. Sometimes that is not easy. Sometimes change sneaks up out of nowhere when we least expect it as it did for me and like it has more recently for many of us. Sometimes that transition is unwanted, so we fight it. Sometimes we're all tangled up in the story that we're telling ourselves about how it's going to be. This can happen even when it's a transition we're excited to be in.

It's easy to forget that we've been here before. From the time we're born, we are faced with one new experience after another. Every time we have moved into a new phase of our life, we've walked into the unknown. Every time we set out to learn something new, we marinated in the transitional space between having no idea what we're doing and mastering it. Every. Single. Time. Along the way, we carve out our comfort zones, and the unknown can become a scary and shadowy space. We completely forget that, really, we've experienced change and transition enough times that we've also amassed many ways to manage it, some of which will now come in quite handy. If we were to put a different lens on this for a moment, we could stop obsessing about the whats and the hows long enough to leverage the one thing that we do know something about: ourselves. Our bodies and our brains have everything we need.

WHAT IS THIS TRANSITION IN YOUR LIFE CALLING YOU TO BE?

Which parts of yourself do you need to call upon to enjoy and find the opportunities as you move from Point A to Point B? What is this transition, this opportunity, this new fork in the road asking from you now? Often, we focus on what we need to be doing or what needs to get done, and in what order. We make lists of tasks. We want the map. We consult the experts about what they did. We avoid just being who we are and asking ourselves who we are being called to grow into next.

What if it were, though, all about who we are *being*? I invite you to slow down, turn your focus away from all the doing and trying to predict the future, and refocus instead on what is happening right here and now, in the present. When you can slow down and be in the present, you can actually accelerate your ability to create deeper and more sustainable changes. When you're standing present, who do you need to be? Of course, we all need support at times when the ground under us is shifting and we are still learning (or building) what's next. But why not start with ourselves first?

Who do you need to be right now to navigate what you are creating next?

Who would you be if you let your unique natural strengths handle this?

You have made successful transitions before. What did it take?

Who are you being when you allow yourself to be led by your core values?

When your future vision becomes reality, how will you be different?

A FEW THINGS YOU CAN STOP DOING

When I was starting my business many years ago, a friend cautioned me not to use the word reinvention because she thought that it would scare people. The concept is too big, she said. It's scary, and it sounds really hard. So let's get this out of the way right now. Yes, reinvention, and any kind of change, can be big and sometimes scary and sometimes it is hard to come alongside that.

It's also exactly what I find a lot of people are craving or working toward. Sometimes, this requires a few tweaks or a change of perspective before some of the hard work, that bigness, actually starts taking care of itself. Most often, living a life we love living and doing the work we love doing *does* ask something of us. It asks us to think differently, to dream, to put ourselves to the test of actually going after what we say we want. It requires acting and allowing changes to happen, as well as actively seeking them out. But that's not always about doing more, being more, and having more. In fact, letting go of a few common obstacle habits will open up a lot more space for all of this. At least while you're reading and working through this book, try letting go of the habits that follow if they sound familiar. You can always take them back up later, but I'm sure you won't want to consider that.

OBSESSING ABOUT EVERYTHING YOU HAVE TO DO

When I worked in journalism, a friend routinely called me to commiserate about work she was dreading, how busy her schedule was, and why nothing was getting done. It was exhausting. The more she talked, the more daunting it all seemed. Yet every time she would agree to get off the phone and actually do the things she was avoiding, the tasks were always simpler and less stressful than anticipated. So many of us tend to do this: We talk endlessly about the projects left to do, how busy we are, what our schedule looks like. I'm not suggesting abandoning your responsibilities, but if this is you, consider this: The whole time you're talking about those things, you're not actually *doing* them—and you're not changing what isn't working for you. Instead, you're stealing time and energy from yourself.

FOCUSING ON WHAT YOU DON'T KNOW

Identifying your learning gaps is important (and we'll discuss that in the Redesign section of this book), but unless you're in the process of clarifying who can help you learn something you need to learn or asking for the specific help you know you need, this mind chatter not only wastes your time, it can create feelings of stress, anxiety, and overwhelm almost out of nowhere. Think about this. When has focusing on the obstacles in your path or all of the things you don't yet know or know how to do ever made you feel more capable, confident, and motivated? If it has, I'd love to hear from you, but if not, you can just let this one go.

ROMANTICIZING WHAT YOU'RE GOING TO DO WHEN YOU "HAVE TIME"

A little tough love is in order here. You and I will never suddenly "have more time" unless you and I make executive decisions about where our time is currently going. No one can take control of our time and energy allocation for us. If an action, objective, or goal is truly important to you, then you must put the time for it on your calendar and understand that not doing that is also a choice. If that's not happening, ask yourself why. Look at where you are spending time. Then do it, schedule it, delegate it, or simply remove it from your list without guilt. There's always a possibility that what you are continually delaying is just not that important right now. If it's a "someday maybe" kind of idea, consider keeping a file or notebook of ideas that you may want to revisit at another time. That way, your desires remain alive, and you can come back to them when you have ample space, energy, and commitment.

TALKING NEGATIVELY TO YOURSELF

Nothing good ever comes of this. Reinventing means giving up perfection for perspective and a chance at expanding your worldview. If the tone and the language you're using with yourself is not supporting that process, if it is not the type of tone and language you would use with people you love, it has no place here. Whether it's mind-drama, your inner critic, or self-judgment, it's time to practice rewriting those narratives and letting them go. Rewiring these patterns will go a long way to helping you reinvent your reality in profound and practical ways—and enhance your experience of moving through all of the stages of your reinvention.

WORRYING ABOUT WHAT EVERYONE ELSE IS DOING

Knowing how others have solved problems or tackled similar obstacles can be useful and even provide inspiration. We can always learn something new in almost any circumstance. But we all know when that balance starts to tip. If you find yourself talking more (or worse, complaining) about how other people are conducting their businesses, growing their careers, raising their kids, changing their lifestyles, or spending their money more than you're walking your own path, that's your sign. When you're comparing yourself to the external view you see of others' lives and coming up short… trouble lies ahead. In yoga, we say, "Keep your eyes on your own mat." The philosophy is simple, and it also requires continual practice. The same holds true here. Having your eyes focused on your own business expands your effectiveness on whatever you are working toward.

Your challenge: As you're going through this book and catch yourself veering into these obstacle habits, gently catch yourself and remember these are the things you no longer need to do. This will be a practice, so you may want to come back to these pages periodically as a reminder.

REINVENTION REMINDERS

- Reinvention is a practice, as well as a process. Take your time and enjoy yourself.

- You can fully expect that when you're creating what's next, there will be feelings, drama, resistance, obstacles, and challenges—along with creativity, joy, excitement, learning, and new results. You are already well-equipped to navigate all of it.

- Creating what's next also means stepping fully present into the new you that you are becoming. Being intentional about how you show up for your life during this time is essential.

- It may sound counterintuitive, but what you let go of throughout the process can streamline your experience and move you forward faster. Obstacle habits and mind chatter are great places to start reinventing by letting go.

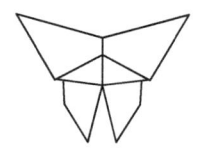

YOUR NEXT STEP

- Answer the questions below about who you are being called to be as you create what's next for your life and your work:

    Who do you need to be right now to navigate what's changing?

    Who would you be if you let your unique natural strengths handle this?

    You have made successful transitions before. What did it take?

    Who are you being when you allow yourself to be led by your core values?

    When your future vision becomes reality, how will you be different?

- Create a *what if...* statement that gives you a new way to look at a pattern that might push you off course and an opening to handle it differently. You'll have this to remind yourself whenever your old pattern comes up (and it will because that's how change works).

- Which of the "obstacle habits" on pages 33-36 feel familiar for you? Which one feels most important to let go of right now?

In the next section, I'll introduce and take you step by step through the Six Stages of Reinvention, beginning with a clear-eyed and honest assessment of where you are, who you are, and what matters most to you in this chapter of your life.

CHAPTER THREE
RECONNECT

THE TIME HAS COME

You've known this for a while now, but maybe you've comfortably settled into a pattern. Perhaps your energy is lagging, and you seem to have less bandwidth and less joy. You're just doing what everyone is doing. Yet your definition of success and fulfillment looks a little different. Work, you imagine, could be more fulfilling. Your career goals and your potential are bigger. There's a lifestyle that you long to create. You want to have more fun, more money, more time, more impact, more... *something*. And so, that part of you begins the search for what's next, for the vision you fully create for yourself.

Reconnection is the first stage of reinvention because it's the foundation on which everything else sits. One of the most common questions I'm asked by clients is what matters most as they find themselves in this space of reassessment. I cannot answer that question. It's your question. Your answer. Your work. Your life. Your vision. But I can show you where to look for the answers. Often, when we're resisting a question or the ways in which we can locate our own answers, it's because we're missing information, like how we really feel, what we really want, what we believe our potential to be. Information like the unique package of strengths that we bring to the world and what is keeping us from doing the work of creating more of what we desire to experience in our life.

It's why, when you're designing your new lifestyle or engineering a change in your work, jumping into action before you've done the homework to assess your inner resources and gain some clarity on where you want to go can actually set you back. Reconnection reveals the difference between the authentic, life-enhancing choice and the reactive, knee-jerk action that keeps you going in circles and questioning your direction. When your work or lifestyle feels ready for big changes, I like to begin with five sets of questions that are designed to start to unearth the missing pieces and reconnect you to the parts of you that are buried under daily life.

> *What's underneath your desire for change? What's going on for you right now, and how is this disconnected from where you really want to be? What is it that you hope these changes will make possible in your life?*
>
> *What's your motivation for taking this on right now, and what is your level of commitment to a change?*
>
> *What are your core values? Values are the non-negotiables in our lives, the foundational pieces that make us uniquely who we are and inform what we hold to be deeply important. This is a question that we rarely ask when life is happening how we think it should be, and yet it's the question that can arguably have the biggest impact on our life and work if we answer it and design accordingly.*
>
> *Where do your strengths lie? What are you naturally best at? How can you identify these strengths and more fully*

develop them so that you're living and working in your natural energetic peaks?

What are your priorities? While we hear similar messages about what we should be prioritizing (success, career, money, family, to name a few), the reality is that we each have a different set of answers, and those priorities are subject to change. Honor what is true for you now, in this season of your life. There are no wrong answers.

What would you do if you felt clear and confident? If you felt confident, if you knew that no one was judging you, if you had permission, if you knew you'd be wildly successful, if you knew that you would be supported, what would you do? It's time to understand what's tugging at you and why.

YOUR FOUNDATION AND CURRENT REALITY

If there's one thing that we all have in common, it's this: Everyone benefits from having a strong foundation from which to launch their dreams, goals, and lives. Every goal, every career transition, and every life change becomes easier when we have solid ground under our feet. When this foundation is strong, we can accomplish more. We can create, connect, and grow more fully. What's truly revolutionary is that we are the ones who can create that solid ground for ourselves. Of course, a strong and solid base—like any upgrade in our lives—doesn't get built in a day. It's created every day, over time. We create it with the habits that make us resilient, the small practices that feed our spirit, the way we nourish our bodies and our minds. Our everyday practices can help build us up, or they can be the things that stand in our way.

A critical component of the Reconnect pillar is to inventory and understand where you are right now. What is your foundation made of? Where is it solid, and where might it need to be shored up for the journey you're about to undertake? The old adage "it's the little things that matter most" is really true here. Every day, we're building or eroding the foundation on which we stand. With all the volatility the world has to offer us, it feels more important than ever to be building this strong base in our own lives. To start, we're going to clear space so that you can reconnect with the largest pieces of your foundation: your strengths, values, resources, and priorities.

START FRESH BY CLEARING OUT WHAT'S NOT WORKING

If there's a lot that's not working right now, this clearing might take time; it might just require making a few simple tweaks. What matters most is that you identify what needs to be cleared out or renegotiated and have the courage to begin. Clearing out physical clutter can be a great metaphor and entry point to begin thinking along these lines. Then you can tackle schedules, situations, commitments, attitudes, media inputs, habitual thinking, and other situations or habits that are draining your energy. If your brain and your environment are feeling cluttered, that's the first sign you need to give your life a good clean sweep so that you can open up space for more of what will support you.

REASSESS HOW YOU'RE SPENDING YOUR TIME

We often think we don't have time to invest in ourselves or even just to BE. We do. We just need to be intentional about carving it out from daily life. Whether you're trying to create a more sustainable and balanced work-life or wanting to make bigger, faster progress on a dream, taking a clear-eyed inventory of where your hours are going will make a difference. It's rarely a lack of time getting in our way; it's almost always that where we're spending our time needs shifting. We have 24 hours every day, and bringing mindfulness to where those hours are being spent allows us to make (sometimes challenging) choices about how we want to use them. This is not about maximizing productivity but intentionality. While training as a coach, one of my mentors challenged me with an extreme version of this exercise. She asked me to inventory where I was spending my time every day and remove 50% of the commitments on my calendar so that I had time to show up fully and immerse myself in the learning. My first response was that this was impossible; I had a very full schedule. With a little work, I did it. As a result, I was able to both commit to my work and absorb the training on a deeper level—and I have never looked at my calendar the same way. I encourage you to take a week or two to document where your time is going and evaluate that against your priorities as you continue through this book. I promise that putting your attention here will motivate changes of some kind. To make it simple, I've included a worksheet for this in the Reinvent Your Reality workbook. (See page 176 for the link and QR code.)

UNDERSTAND WHERE YOUR ENERGY IS FLAGGING

Like the hours in your day, your personal energy is a finite and precious resource. Sure, you might ramp up your energy levels a bit by fueling yourself wisely (we'll talk more about how to do that in Chapter 5), but your supply is not endless. As with time, you are in charge of what you spend energy on and what you don't, as well as the quality of energy you bring to everything that requires your presence.

Wherever possible, I want you to consider how you can direct more of your energy toward activities, people, situations, and mindsets that fuel, not drain, you. You may already sense what feels draining to you, and now you'll bring mindful attention to this. Pull out your phone or a piece of paper and jot down at least ten things that drain your energy. These will be prime opportunities for elimination as you move through the work in this chapter. If there are one or more items that you can eliminate immediately, I encourage you not to wait. Get that energy flowing!

RAISE OR LOWER YOUR STANDARDS

Often, the common wisdom is that ratcheting up our personal and professional expectations is the key to feeling more revitalized and fulfilled in our lives and careers. Brain scan research has shown, in fact, that reaching toward a bigger vision can motivate us in very effective ways. What often gets left out of this discussion, though, is that sometimes expectations and high standards can also keep you stuck. This is especially true if you tend toward perfectionist behavior. In that case, what can often propel you forward is to drop your standards down a notch, slow down, and allow for the perfectly good on the way to excellence and mastery. As you reconnect to yourself and your current reality, you might find that your standards need to be raised, lowered, or accepted for where they are.

LISTEN TO WHAT YOU'RE TELLING YOURSELF

Humans are natural storytellers. We use stories to make sense of our experiences and share them with others; we also act out of the stories we tell throughout our lives. As you slow down enough to hear, examine, and even challenge what you are thinking or believe about a situation, you engage in a transformative practice that puts solid ground under your feet.

BUILD RITUALS AND ROUTINES

A morning routine puts a time-based foundation under the rest of your day. This is true of any of the small rituals, habits, and routines you engage in every day, and this is their power. Choosing small acts that consistently reconnect you to yourself and your life is a cornerstone of creating real balance and a foundation for making bigger life or career changes. Think about the daily or weekly actions you engage in currently. Where do they nurture you, reconnect you, and set you up for success, however you define that term? What is missing that you might like to incorporate?

When you pay attention and take inspired, consistent action to put a healthy foundation under everything you do, you will naturally build the structure you need to shift your well-being, goals, and growth into a place of higher priority. You find the power to tell the truth about your experience instead of holding back. Standing more solidly on your own ground allows you to better hear and use your own voice. Solid foundations help you evolve into a more confident, connected version of yourself. Imagine what might be possible from that place that wasn't possible before. We are going to find out!

OWN WHAT IS TRUE FOR YOU

Another key part of a solid foundation is investing the time to know yourself better. In this chapter, we're going to explore and embrace key aspects of you—your strengths, values, and priorities—to give you clarity and honesty about what you want and need. This is the time to embrace the priorities that matter most to you, allow your inner self to shine brightly, and gain clarity about who you are and want to be. Reconnecting may feel like a lot of excavation work, and it can be. Spending the time to rejoin these important parts of yourself will also streamline your decision-making and open up possibilities for more alignment and fulfillment in your life and work.

What truly matters to you at this point in your life? There are many high ideals worth laying claim to and orienting our lives around. Who among us doesn't say loved ones are most important, that love and justice matter, or that we value hard work and honest people? Our core values are those that we wouldn't be without, regardless of circumstance. They define who we are being every day and can drive the choices we make on a deep level.

Values show up in our lives in different ways—and all reinventions must take them into account. When you start to design your life around your individual values, everything becomes simpler. Decision-making is easier when you are clear on what's most important to you. Value conflicts are more obvious and easier to untangle and navigate. When you can identify and clearly articulate what matters most to you, you're connected with something bigger than the day-to-day concerns that ordinarily dominate the day. With a strong anchor to your values, you can sink deeper into your life because you are grounded in who you are and what matters most to you.

When I work with clients to excavate and clarify their values, I include the philosophical orientation they bring to those values. For example, several of my clients name "accomplishment" as a core value, but how that value manifests itself in their lives is quite different because they see the meaning differently. To one, accomplishment is expressed by building a lucrative career so that he can retire early and follow other passions. Another client defines accomplishment as becoming so known for her work that she can choose only to take on contracts or projects with clients who share her values. A third client prioritizes her value of accomplishment by investing in building generational wealth to expand her children's options. Those are just three of many potential orientations to the value of accomplishment.

At the end of this chapter, you will have the opportunity to identify your values and how they currently show up in your life and career. Invest some quality time with this rather than rushing through it. You might consider doing a values study on how you tracked your time to see where these values are present (or lacking) in your daily life. Drilling down to what is most essential is an enlightening process, and our values tend to reveal themselves in more nuance over time. Building a values-based life means getting very clear on what matters to you on a core level and why.

RECONNECTING TO YOUR STRENGTHS

Natural strengths are another foundational ingredient for building what's next. Where are you at your best? We all have natural abilities, gifts, ways of being, and talents that come easily to us. You might easily identify these strengths as the tasks you find easy and maybe overlook because they're "just who you are." That's an excellent starting point for identifying your strengths. Like core values, strengths are an anchor to well-being. Research increasingly shows that developing your strengths is linked to positive outcomes and can be an important anchor to building a more fulfilling and vital life and career. Even when working on their own to identify and develop their natural strengths, respondents in one Gallup study self-reported that they were making better choices and felt more productive and self-confident. Strengths amplify our energy and create ripples that enhance positivity, productivity, performance, life balance, and other critical components of successful reinvention.

Too often, though, when developing our career or a new framework for our life, we tend to focus on what's missing and improving qualities we wish we had or skills we were better at doing. However, the "needs improvement" section of your performance review is not the foundation for what's next for you. To revitalize your life and work, let's set aside the collective obsession with self-improvement and turn your focus to where it is most positive and effective: leveraging and building upon your successes, what gives you energy, and what you are naturally great at doing.

Research has also shown that this strengths-based approach helps us handle transitions with less stress and more resilience, aids in more effective decision-making, and increases subjective well-being, optimism, and problem-solving capacity. When you understand what your natural strengths are and how you can develop them to greater capacity, you can leverage these effects, too. Most of us have a broad picture of the things we believe we are skilled and not skilled at doing. A more comprehensive strengths view, though, also reflects the activities and capacities that give you energy rather than drain you.

What strengths are you currently using in your work and your life? Are there strengths that you would love to use more? Often, the stress points in our lives point us to where we are operating from draining behaviors we've learned because of circumstance or weaker areas that are not our natural strengths. Likewise, stress points can also point to places where you are over-relying on a particular strength and may need to modulate how and when you use it. Whether you take a formal assessment, work with a coach to identify your strengths, or assess them in a more informal way, your strengths are one of the most important components of your foundation. At the end of this chapter, you will have the opportunity to explore your strengths from several perspectives.

BUILDING IN BALANCE FROM THE START

No matter which area of our life we're working on changing and developing, that effort impacts the whole of our life, starting from the moment we begin. We don't exist as dual humans who have a personal self and a professional self, yet so much of our approach to change and transition—and to developing our contribution in the world—is built on that myth. That's why it's critical to evaluate your current and desired life balance as you reconnect to yourself, your life, and the elements that are important for you to feel and perform at your best.

This shift starts with clarity about the current situations in your own life and your desired feeling of balance. It's completely unnecessary and counterproductive to take on definitions and expectations of balance that do not fit you or your life, whether in your current reality or the desired one. It's *your* integrity that you want to fully stand inside, not the larger world's. One of the most important things you can do as you reinvent your own reality is define what balance means in your own life and begin to set up structures that will allow you to claim that for yourself.

Achieving real-life balance isn't a one-and-done operation, but it is certainly far from impossible. In fact, it's the natural state that we are designed for; our human bodies work best when we are in a balanced and sustainable state. We see this in how the brain responds to rest or downtime by creating more synchrony. The brain's default mode network (DMN), well studied for its role in daydreaming and mental processing, is one of numerous resting networks regulating everything from memory to vision. Your brain is always trying to create homeostasis within your physical body systems. As psychologist and neuroscientist Lisa Feldman Barrett shares in her book, *Seven and a Half Lessons About the Brain*, our brains are innately designed to manage physical and mental deposits and withdrawals to keep us in balance. They are always balancing a budget, so to speak.

We'll talk more about how to bring your definitions of wellness and balance into reality in Chapter 5. For now, consider that comprehensive wellness and fulfillment rely on balance, and the job of defining or allowing balance in our lives is one that cannot effectively be delegated. As with most things worth doing, this requires growing into and setting significant boundaries about your priorities, energy, and time.

As you work through the reconnection process, be sure to consider your state of balance and examine any thoughts that may have you operating within someone else's idea of what balance means or not having balance at all. Here are a few questions you may wish to consider or bring to your journal:

What do you currently believe about balance?

What does it really mean to you to be living a balanced life?

What boundaries have you set around balance, and where are those boundaries working and not working?

Where does your life feel integrated, and where is integration lacking?

What are the priorities in this season of your life, and what may be less important right now?

What new boundaries might you need to set as you design what's next for you?

PAINT A PICTURE OF YOUR SKILLS AND INTERESTS

If the parts of your life that you're ready to reinvent involve your career, business, or vocation, it's likely that your initial thoughts about what's next started with your professional skillset and interests. Career advisors often start here as well. I purposely place skills and interests at the end of the Reconnect process because, while they are important, my experience is that when we're clear on the more foundational parts of ourselves, we tend to view our skills and interests differently.

In thinking about your interests, it's helpful to cast a wide net. Just as fulfillment and meaning don't always come from work, the workplace isn't the only place where you are building and honing valuable skills. Everything you are involved with shapes your skills and interests. Many of us have personal interests that have fueled personal growth, brought us a feeling of connection and belonging, and taught us new skills or developed ones that we already had. For example, you might have fulfilling volunteer roles or community engagement that helped you develop skills that have little to do with your job. If you think about your skills and interests together and divide them into a couple of specific buckets, you gain a clearer picture of everything you bring to the table.

Soft, or relational, skills are the intangible skillsets that you bring to everything you do, and because they inform much of what you do, they can, in some cases, be more important than the learned technical skills that relate to your job. This bucket includes skills such as creativity, critical thinking, emotional intelligence, relationship building, networking, mentoring, strategy, and more.

Professional and technical skills are the skills you may have been trained in or learned on the job, those related to your specific line of work. These may include your actual job functions, past and present, specific technical knowledge, technology and computer proficiencies, and more.

In exploring your skillset, you also want to consider any formal or informal training you might have, whether that is education, on-the-job training, professional development courses and certificates, or training through non-work-related organizations.

Outside of the obvious result of the training, what else did it require of you? What did you learn, and what did you develop as a result of that training? For example, to complete a graduate degree while working and managing a family, you may have developed keen organizational and time management skills just to make it all work—those skills are valuable assets!

Now, let's explore your personal and professional interests. Since this book is founded on a "whole life" philosophy, I highly encourage casting a wide net here and looking at what draws your attention, what you can talk about for hours, what you love to do, when you lose track of time—in all areas of your life. Don't leave anything out, even if it feels completely irrelevant at the moment. We are taking a full inventory of you. Use these questions to get you started:

> *What are the personal interests that hold meaning and value for you?*
>
> *What could you talk about or research for hours? What about that topic holds your attention?*
>
> *What do you most love to read about, watch television or movies about, or listen to?*

How would you like to incorporate those interests going forward?

While taking post-graduate coursework, I learned a point about creativity and innovation that has always stuck with me and that I have used for many years in my coaching work. In the course and the book, *In Genius: A Crash Course on Creativity*, Professor Tina Seelig notes that innovation and creative thinking can often be the result of two unlike things merging together. That's what we're doing here. When you combine your interests with the knowledge and skills you have developed throughout your life to date, you can often come up with new ideas and unearth unexpected potential paths to explore. Even if two colliding skills and interests don't reveal a new path, they will expand your thinking and give you a deeper appreciation of the well of skills and interests you have to share with the world and how they fit into your life as a whole. So be sure not to leave anything out. You can start with these questions:

Where are the creative connections you can see between your various interests?

Where might you combine two unrelated interests?

Where could you employ a current skillset in a new area of interest or a longtime interest with a skillset that you've recently developed?

What patterns do you notice about your skills, interests, or both?

REINVENTION REMINDERS

- To build your foundation, start with a deep dive into who you are and the current realities of what's working and not working for you. Be honest! When you do this, you open up more possibilities for creating a next-level life that is more satisfying.

- Everything you want to create benefits from sitting on a strong and well-designed foundation. As you reassess your time, energy, life, and work priorities, values, strengths, interests, and skillsets, you identify the resources you already have in place, what you want to build upon, and what to let go of.

- It can be tempting to skip the Reconnect stage and jump into planning mode. Don't get ahead of yourself by skipping over what is arguably the most important work you will do. Deepening your self-knowledge and connecting to your current reality makes everything that comes next easier and more cohesive.

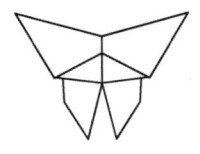

YOUR NEXT STEP

- Spend the time to reconnect to where you are now, particularly in the following areas:

    Time and energy.

    Values.

    Strengths.

    Interests and priorities.

    Skillset.

- Download and take the values assessment included in the online workbook. What do the results and the process tell you about what really matters to you?

- Name three of your top strengths that could help you move toward what's next for you. Go deeper with a formal assessment such as the VIA Character Strengths Survey, Strengths Profile, or the Clifton StrengthsFinder.

- Make a list of your top skills and interests.

- Take inventory of your quality and focus areas of your life as it stands right now.

- Links to all of the resources and assessments mentioned here can be found at www.wholelifestrategies.com/ryrworkbook or scan the QR code on page 176.

Now that you have a clear sense of where you are, what is working and not working, and the most foundational parts of you, you're ready to think bigger about what is possible for you. It's time to reimagine.

CHAPTER FOUR
REIMAGINE

EVERYTHING STARTS AS A THOUGHT

In launching any kind of change, it's helpful to start with the end in mind but not just any end. To fully engage your motivation and creative thinking, research in the field of neuroscience and coaching shows that you can move more effectively toward your goals when you're working toward the end that deeply matters to you. That's not always the most obvious end, though, so in the Reimagine stage, we start with a 30,000-foot view of what you want, what truly matters to you, and how you'd love your life to look.

In this chapter, you will envision and begin to inhabit the end result of the changes you want to make. You'll examine your goals in the context of the bigger dream you have for your life and the experiences that you want to create for yourself. This is the space to be honest with yourself about all of your desires, even the ones that don't make sense right now or feel out of reach. Building on what you've learned in the Reconnect stage, you'll get clear on not just what but why.

WHAT DO YOU REALLY, REALLY WANT?

For many of us, this question has been more of an afterthought. It's been unclear or unexpected to ask. How often have you really thought about the answer? It's important to note that we're talking about what *you* want, not what your manager, your spouse, your parents, your friends, or even your dog wants for you (though it's probably safe to say man's best friend doesn't have much of an agenda). When you're honest about what you really want and focus your resources and integrity in the direction of achieving that, you create more fulfillment and happiness to spread around to others in your life. So think about this question carefully. What do you really, really want? What do you want to change, to accomplish, to continue, experience, or contribute?

These can be challenging questions, especially if you don't yet know how you're going to get there. But if you aren't asking the questions, you won't get clear answers. When I was first starting out as a coach, I thought I had answered these questions clearly. I was creating my answers! Then, during a three-day training event, I was asked to dig deeper. I was asked, "What do you really, really want?" for a period of several minutes. As the seconds clicked by, I wasn't let off the hook. The person who asked listened intently and continued: *And what else, and what else, and what else.* It felt like an eternity. When you're not practiced with opening up to your desires, shining a spotlight on them can feel uncomfortable. It can take time to get clear and fully honest with yourself.

What happens when you ask yourself what you really want? What if you asked a friend or a partner and (this is the critical piece) really made space for hearing and acknowledging their desires? What happens when you don't settle for the first answer? What if you keep asking until the list is a mile long and years into the future? Does answering the question of what you want feel uncomfortable for you? If so, that's not unusual. Many of us share a belief system that holds wants and desires as less than, unsavory, or—worse—just not allowed. We may have been taught that we are not supposed to want but to focus on only what we need, especially when others elsewhere might be struggling or when we have others to care for. At the very least, I find that when we are wanting, in many cases, we're not wanting out loud or expansively.

If that's you, I want to challenge your thinking around what you really want and why it's not only OK to go there, it's essential. Consider this: Without the desire, nothing gets accomplished in this world. Nothing small and nothing large. Desire causes action. It mobilizes resources. It brings people together, and it changes the world. The world's greatest social changes, inventions, and developments happened because somebody wanted them. More often, a lot of somebodies wanted them. Sometimes that change happens in our own world first, but it always has ripple effects. The most impactful positive changes in our lives come when we truly want them and know why we want them. In most cases, they involve results that no one else can get for us; we must step forward and honor the desire *simply because we want it*.

As a side note, many of us who were socialized as women or in marginalized communities have been culturally conditioned to put our wants and desires aside for centuries. That time has passed. There is creative power in your true desires, so let's uncover them and make them reality. It's also entirely possible that wanting is not a selfish act. We don't simply want for ourselves. We can want for everybody. After you've experimented with this deep brainstorming, sit quietly and document everything you came up with so that you can revisit your ideas later when you start to plan and redesign. I still keep a list like this, or rather a whole box of cards, in my home office, transferring the items I'm currently working on into my planner to focus my attention. The rest are sitting there for when I'm ready.

As you work through this chapter, I invite you to spend some quality time with these questions.

> *What is it that you really, really want?*
>
> *And what do you want for others?*
>
> *In your life?*
>
> *For your family?*
>
> *In your career?*
>
> *For your community?*
>
> *For future generations?*

Knowing your answers could completely change your life, and that is exactly what we're after.

A PERSONAL NOTE ABOUT FREEDOM

As you start to reimagine the possibilities for what's next, a word that often comes up is "freedom." I'd like to address that because freedom has always been a strong personal value for me, and what I've learned through years of coaching professionals to make meaningful changes in their lives and careers is that it can be a powerful underlying driver of change.

But it's not enough.

When we talk about freedom, we often think of breaking free *from something*. That might be freedom from restrictions on our speech or religion, for example. Or breaking free from oppressive systems and situations. In the context of building what's next for your career, it can mean freedom from the corporate cubicle or schedule, freedom from career expectations that don't fit, or freedom from a restrictive work culture or micromanaging bosses. On the personal side, you might want the freedom of starting over in a new environment, freedom from financial stress, from relationships that aren't working, even from your own sabotaging patterns.

When I embarked on the biggest change period of my life to date, my intention was to free myself from daily reminders of what was essentially a traumatic period in my personal life. I also wanted to be free from the stress of doing the jobs of several people with a limited budget, and not just at work. I imagined being free from going into an office every day and free from the mind drama that I suspected was keeping me from making big decisions. By the time I packed up my office, said goodbye to coworkers who felt like family, packed up my townhouse, canceled my lease, sold a property, and solidified plans to move cross country, a lot had led up to that point. It wasn't spontaneous, simple, or easy. It felt like a big leap into the unknown, and it was. It also felt necessary. I was making decisions based on "freedom from" energy because I wasn't fully clear on what I was moving *toward.*

After a ten-day grounding meditation retreat, I spent a few weeks with my family, finishing up consulting projects at the kitchen table, and felt a time freedom I hadn't felt in years. I'd spent the last three years putting out fires, real and metaphoric. I reveled in the rest. I had always built some amount of schedule and decision-making freedom into every job I'd ever held, but this felt more expansive. I tend to limit clutter and debt in my life because those things have always felt restrictive (and not free) to me. In wiping the slate clean, I was connecting even more dots between my foundational values and what I was doing every day. Of course,

I also felt the mix of excitement and fear that comes with leaving my well-established comfort zone, routines, and communities without knowing what "next" would look like or even what I wanted it to look like.

With my clients, it's often the same. Many talk about wanting freedom from the pressure of trying to juggle all the balls, all the time, or freedom from a work situation or relationship that is depleting their energy or not allowing their true potential to emerge. They may want to feel free not to play by rules that don't make sense to them and aren't getting the results they desire or free from critical, doubtful, fearful voices, and patterns that keep them stuck. There is often a lot of "away" energy.

Freedom, though, is not only a state of leaving behind. It's an expression of what we are *free to* create. It's very much about moving *toward* something. That may look like freedom to build a better life for yourself or your family, freedom to work where and when you prefer, or freedom to make a big leap based on your values and priorities. In time, I came to see that what I really wanted was to feel free to choose after several years of reacting to choices made for and around me. I wanted the freedom to be my own boss, as I'd always secretly desired to be. I imagined the freedom of working where and when I wanted and engaging my creativity in new ways. I craved the freedom to construct more space in my previously crazy-busy life, to travel, to try new things, to reinvent everything that needed reinventing.

My clients tell me they crave these things, too. Underneath the "breaking free from" is always the *freedom to* choose a path that lights them up instead of the one they'd always thought they should follow. Freedom to make their own rules and follow the dream they've been pushing to the back burner. Freedom to carve out the time and energy to fully nourish themselves and their lives, so they can fully show up in the world.

As you start to reimagine new possibilities for your life and work, consider whether you are moving toward or away. As you grow and evolve, what you choose to be free from and what you are free to create evolves, too.

What does the idea of freedom spark in you?

When you begin to reimagine what's next for you, how are the concepts of freedom from and freedom to evolving with you as you develop that vision?

What do you need to release so you can unleash the energy that feels stuck in you?

What do you need to create for yourself to put that energy to work in service of you, your life, work, community, or future endeavors?

YOUR VISION HAS POWER

When you set an intention and spend time creating a clear vision of what you want, life happens differently. Research at the crossroads of coaching and neuroscience at Case Western's Coaching Research Lab continues to show the profound effectiveness of thinking bigger and bolder—expanding beyond the immediate how to reach a goal or fill a gap into the larger dreams for our lives. Setting and solving problem-based goals that we are then held accountable to achieve on a specific, short-term timeline activates a completely different part of the brain.

In other words, goals are most effective when they're tied to a bigger picture of who we want to be and what we want to achieve, or what Dr. Richard Boyatzis at Case Western calls the "ideal self." When you tap into this larger view of your life and who you will be in that life, the brain activates to encourage more creative thinking, positive emotion, and a natural motivation that helps you create more of what you want.

Contrast that with a typical goal-setting exercise based on a three-year plan to achieve milestones that you expect of yourself or performance-based goals that others expect of you. This "should-based" approach can trigger stress hormones in the nervous system and encourage the brain to activate in a different way altogether. In Boyatzis' research, this more traditional goal-setting performance-based approach is called "coaching for compliance" and is related to the "ought self," the person you are when you're weighted with expectation and obligation, whether from others or yourself.

Setting a bigger vision and intention for our life is not magical thinking that generates magic results. Strategy and planning have a place in the mix as you put the pieces of your vision into action. That action is much harder, though, when you haven't done the first things first to set your brain up for success. In business, successful companies often build their strategy around a blue-sky vision and an impactful mission. They have a sense of where they are headed before they start heading there. Yet what seems like common business sense can get lost in translation when looking at our own individual lives. Similarly, many elite athletes rely on visualization practices—imagining and immersing themselves in seeing the ultimate outcome—to reach seemingly impossible goals. These tools have deep relevance for reinventing anything in your life.

To fully put these phenomena and the science behind them to work, immerse yourself in your own 30,000-foot view. Then, to fully expand your thinking and activate the personal emotional attractor system within your brain, imagine your life and your career to be even bigger and more wonderful than you initially thought. Imagine what would feel like the ideal scenario to you. Then expand it. And expand it again.

Whether you are focused on changing your mindset to imagine a positive result to a difficult life situation or reimagining the possibilities for changing careers, when you are grounded in what you intend to happen within a bigger dream you envision for your life, you will begin to notice changes that sneak in so stealthily that they seem to happen on their own. Sometimes it feels like synchronicity. Sometimes we don't make the connection. Always, your vision activates change.

With that clearer vision, you can also begin to act differently, see differently, and connect new ideas. The impossible seems more possible. When you focus on that vision of what you really want, pieces of that vision become more visible to you in your daily life. When you believe in an ideal outcome, those outcomes are more likely to unfold, even if they aren't in the exact form you were expecting. This is the space where synchronicities unfold, where mindset shifts can "suddenly" resolve stuck situations, and where seemingly unmanageable timing falls neatly into place. This philosophy has proven itself in my own life and in the lives of many of my clients and colleagues. Much of what I once thought "impossible" became not just possible; it became the new normal, raising the ceiling for what's next. That's what reinvention mindset is all about. That's the power of thinking differently about your career and your life as a whole.

Once you've had plenty of time to expand your vision, consider how you can immerse yourself within it in tangible, practical ways and start to break it down to the smallest steps. What parts of that vision can you do, have, or be right now? How would you like to show up in your life today? What would you like to experience as you go through your day? Spend a few minutes with this every morning. During the day, make the effort to pay attention to what happens, what you notice, and how you're feeling. Watch for movement.

> *What does your expanded vision look like?*
>
> *What values would you like to live into more fully?*
>
> *What strengths would you like to develop more fully?*
>
> *What interests are calling to you to explore further?*
>
> *What could you add to your vision of the future that would support those strengths, values, and interests?*
>
> *How can you "be there now" and embody even the smallest piece of what you're becoming?*

INTENDING MEANING FROM THE START

One of the factors that spurs us into reimagining what we want for our lives (and our work in the world as one essential part of that life) is a desire to connect our daily experience to meaningful action and dreams. Living a life with meaning is not a one-size-fits-all prescription, however. What is meaningful to me, for example, may not be infused with the same level of meaning for you, and it's important to take a clear-eyed look at this during the Reimagine stage of any reinvention that you feel ready to undertake.

Definitions of meaning are complex and comprise a number of

factors. The typical routines and actions of your day can enhance or detract from your feeling of meaning, as can your relationships and community connections. Then there's alignment: How well does your current life and work meet your internal and external needs, for example, or how do your values connect to where your time is going every day? Sorting your own criteria for what is meaningful for you takes a concerted effort to identify what feels most impactful for you. In looking at what is personally meaningful for you, there are no right answers. Put aside any factors that fall into the categories of things you think you are supposed to find meaning in, that you feel you "should" want to incorporate into your life and work, and any other external pressures or narratives about what meaning is and what it isn't.

Finding the sweet spot of your own meaning-making is an internal process that requires permission to be authentically you, not from anyone else, but yourself. Like most deep dives into who we want to be versus who we think we're expected to be, this one might mean sitting with it while you come to answers that spark that sense of real connection within you.

This integrity exercise might be one you want to come back to more than once. I encourage you to complete it at least once before moving into Chapter 5 and to revisit it when you've completed a few of the experiments in Chapter 7. Testing our ideas and visions with real-world experiments usually provides additional information about what really matters and what we can move to a lower priority or let go of altogether.

In the Reimagine stage, let your expansive thinking take you out of what you know and dream into how you would ideally measure what's meaningful for you if you were creating it from scratch. For the purposes of this chapter, that is what you are doing. Allow your mind to relax, dream, and reimagine your most meaningful life.

A few questions you may want to consider as you complete this chapter include:

> If I were to rank my top five ingredients of meaning, what's the ranking? What might be the next five?

> Where have these ingredients been obvious in my decision-making? Where have they been neglected?

> How do my ingredients for meaning map over to my strengths, values, and needs?

> If I were to imagine a vision for my future that was infused with my own definition of meaning, what would that look like, and what would I be experiencing?

A VISION THAT PULLS YOU FORWARD

Now that you're honest about what you really want and what truly matters to you let's take it a step further. When you've made the changes you want to make, how will your life be different? Have fun with this question. Get juicy with the details and put yourself right into the scene. When I work with clients on this, I often ask them to feel their way into this future vision rather than to just think their way through it. What will your future life *feel* like? What will you be experiencing? What are the visual images that come to mind? What do you sense?

Let your visioning be a full-body experience instead of an intellectual exercise, too. One way to do this is to imagine yourself in a scenario that represents your ideal vision. Without words, notice what's happening within your body, what you feel and sense. As you tune into the details, stay with these sensations. As you notice what's missing or what you would add, stay with your full sensory awareness. You may choose to write a story of your experience, represent your vision with art, record yourself talking your way through it—whatever feels most natural to you. However you tell the story of your ideal vision, try to stay connected to the physical feelings it evokes in you.

Bringing your body sensations into the process of articulating your vision creates an embodied knowing that integrates your vision into body and mind. In other words, it puts the whole of you to work for what you want to create. It's so much harder to have and enjoy what you most want—whether that's a feeling, a relationship, a job, a schedule, an outcome, or a material desire—when you aren't even sure what it looks and feels like. Without spending the time to fully reimagine, you may find that this piece or that piece does fall into place as you stumble along in default mode. But you may also waste time with a lot of things that aren't such a good fit. I have been there myself, and this experience can lull you into a comfortable feeling that quiets your knowing and intuition about what is missing. You can wake yourself from this kind of sleepwalking through daily life by taking abstract thoughts or musings about what you want your life to look like and making it real to you.

My training and personal experience are that the values-based vision at the heart of the Reimagine stage is central to how you move forward with reinventing anything. That isn't to say that even your most vividly imagined future vision won't change. It will very likely change and evolve as you do, but the act of fully inhabiting the vision is your opening. You're opening the door to everything that comes next and connecting all of the pieces of you into a beautiful tapestry of possibility. Here are a few ways to do it:

- Mind mapping. Are you a stream of consciousness thinker, a visual learner, or a list maker? Try diagramming your thoughts in a mind map on paper or by using an online mind mapping tool.

- Journaling. If you enjoy writing or keeping a journal, write a vivid, detailed description of your vision of your life "afterward."

- Imagining. Many people, including high-performance athletes, creatively visualize their ideal outcome before it happens. If this appeals to you, set aside time to thoroughly imagine what it feels like to achieve what you're working toward.

- Sharing. If you are someone who needs to talk things through, schedule time with a trusted and supportive friend, colleague, or loved one and tell them all about your vision.

- Future self. Draft an email to yourself, written by the future you on the day when you've achieved your desired outcome, and fully describe how life looks "on the other side."

What's the real role of spending this time to reimagine your life and map out a vision? You're giving yourself direction and the gift of feeling empowered, inspired, nurtured, and hopeful. You're building a solid foundation under your goals and creating a life roadmap that resonates with you on a deep level.

YOUR NEXT CHAPTER

From the time I began coaching, I have based much of my work with clients around a framework I call "dream it, design it, live it," which is exactly what it sounds like. The Six Stages of Reinvention evolved from this work. It really doesn't matter whether the focus is a complete lifestyle overhaul, a deep dive into what's next at work, or sustainable strategies to reach that long-postponed big hairy audacious goal (as author Jim Collins terms it), this underlying philosophy always gets results.

At the heart of how we do each of these three things—dream, design, and thrive—is story. That's because there are few things more foundational to our experience of life than the stories we tell ourselves and others. The words we use matter, and so do the narratives we build with them. Our stories influence what we see, how we show up, where we show up, what actions we take, even what we believe to be possible. What quickly becomes clear is that our stories aren't facts. No matter how deeply ingrained they may be or how much we cling to them for their familiarity, they are just narratives. And as any reader or writer knows, every storyline is open to be examined, critiqued, revised, thrown out, recast, or improved upon.

I've been a writer my whole life, so crafting a story is something that naturally resonates with me as a coach and as a human. What I've learned, though, is psychology backs me up here. Our brains are always creating stories, trying to make meaning from our experiences. The multiple parts of our brain biology are constantly scanning our environment, internally and externally, for cues on how they should respond. As these multiple areas interpret and respond, they rise and fall in dominance and harmony, working much like an orchestra. With awareness and effort, we can better understand our brains, which areas are telling which stories, and better understand the stories we live by. As we reimagine, we're actively creating stories with the goal of ultimately making them serve us better.

This is why I like to conclude the reimagine work with a new, reimagined story based on your vision, your factors of meaning, and anything else you want to add to it. Here's how you can assess the stories you may be operating in right now and wrap your reimagining into a brand-new story, one that will guide you to your next chapter.

DISCOVER

Stepping back long enough to question the "facts" of your experience can reveal stories you may want to keep or discard. Once you have a bit of distance and awareness, you can begin to sort through them, question them, and ultimately transform what needs transforming. When you identify a story that needs reinventing, it is not "wrong," even if it's not "true." It likely does serve a purpose. It might represent an important lesson waiting to be completed, an outdated way of managing stressors, or a doorway to upgrading your life. These stories might offer a clue as to where your next area of focus needs to be. They may also hold the resolution to a longstanding concern. Examine them from all angles because the one thing your stories are not is you.

DISSECT

This is the empowering part. As soon as you can see your own stories and stuck places, you have opened up brand-new choices. Seeing them for what they are puts you back in the driver's seat. Knowing what you now know, what would you like to do about these narratives that have been present in your life? There might be a better, more inspiring story that is equally true, for example. It's time to dissect the story that's embedded in you as a book reviewer might. Does this story hold up? Is it really that interesting? Who are the important characters, the villains and heroes? What's the plot? With every new story comes new strategies, new ways of being, new possibilities, and new action plans. Knowing which actions, attitudes, and ways of being align with your new, more empowering story is how you begin to write a new narrative in your life, how you create a new vision, a new chapter, a new set of standards—one little story at a time.

DELIBERATE RESPONSE

Deliberately choosing your responses sounds like a simple process, but living into your new stories does take practice. It takes time, and it takes choice. Instead of reacting to a bad day at work with a story about how terrible your boss is and how you need to get out of there, you might instead stop for a minute, breathe, and remember that you are the storyteller here. If you're the victim in this story, for example, your reaction is going to be different than if your character is the person who overcame the challenge of a difficult day or learned something valuable about the kind of work you now want to be doing and not doing. In these moments of awareness and narrative choice, the automatic reactions you're used to can start to give way to more deliberate and effective ways of responding to everything around you. You're equipping yourself to make real choices in the moment about which actions give life to the story you want to be living: your vision for what's next.

DESIGN

As you can see, reimagining your life through the lens of story opens up an amazing amount of possibility. But how do you become the person who is actually living that version of your life? This is where having a clear vision, strong standards, and designing your mindset, action plans, support systems, and environments all come into play. But we don't have to go there quite yet. First, experiment with what it's like to change roles, write a new chapter in your life, or tell a story that pulls you into a happier way of being. When you regularly practice putting yourself into new roles or new storylines, notice how that feels and keep on experimenting. The next thing you know, that new chapter will have arrived.

REINVENTION REMINDERS

- Honest reflection about what you really want is the first step to using your resources and integrity to achieve it. Thinking clearly and courageously about what you really, really want opens the door to sustainable change. If you could create what's next (and you can), what do you truly want to change, to accomplish, to continue?

- Tapping into a big-picture, ideal view of what you want to experience, contribute, and who you want to be in your life activates the brain and encourages creative thinking, positive emotion, and natural motivation, instead of relying on external goals, motivations, and willpower.

- Reinvention often means that we are wanting *freedom from* as well as *freedom to*. It's both about leaving behind and moving toward.

- Living a meaningful life isn't something to stumble upon or leave to chance. Be sure to include an exploration of what is meaningful to you as you create your future vision.

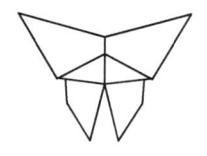

YOUR NEXT STEP

- What do you really, really want? Explore this in a journal or with a friend. Here are two ways to unlock expansive thinking about what you want to be, do, have, and experience:

    - Set aside 10-15 minutes of quiet time and write your answer to this question. If you get stuck, keep asking and write whatever comes to mind.

    - Schedule 10-15 minutes with a trusted person so they can ask you this question. They can write or record whatever you say so you have documentation. If you get stuck, they can prompt you with "what else?" but ask them not to comment or react; just listen.

- Explore the questions on page 70 to help you identify the ingredients that are most meaningful for you.

- Complete your vision statement using whichever tool or tools you like from the list on pages 72.

Now that we've identified where you are and an inspiring dream for what could be possible for you, let's pause to explore another critical piece of your reinvention foundation: what will revitalize or nourish you for the journey.

CHAPTER FIVE
REVITALIZE

THRIVING, NOT SURVIVING

Change is not always easy, even when we're working hard to create it. What often happens when we start to expand our possibilities and dream a bigger vision for our lives is that our ego and habitual ways of being can step in and start to create discomfort and anxiety and throw up a fair amount of resistance. This is why there needs to be an interim step between the creative, expansive work of creating a vision that truly pulls you forward into what you'd like to create next and the actual design work of developing a clear plan to make that happen.

I call this critical stage Revitalize because it is this important work that infuses our dreams with the vitality and energy we need to architect changes and to fuel our mental, physical, emotional, and environmental capacities to help us in building what we say we want to create. I strongly encourage you not to skip the work in this chapter, even if you have implemented reasonable self-care practices and don't feel like your energy is lagging. While reinventing may not be complicated, it does require work, time, energy, creativity, and boundary setting with yourself and others.

The stronger and more resourced you are going in, the better your experience and your results will be.

In this chapter, we will examine how to develop a strong foundation of meaningful self-care and energy management under you so that you are operating at your best. This can be a lifetime's work because we're always growing and evolving, but to help lay the ground for redesigning parts of your life and work, we'll pay particular attention to revitalizing a few key areas that will make a big impact for you right away. If you'd like to take this work even deeper, I recommend checking out my book *Nourish: 28 Daily Dares for Busy People Craving Sustainable Self-Care* to help you solidify your personal foundation and create meaningful self-care practices that fit into a busy life.

As we dive into your self-care reality and make some adjustments, we'll use a balanced, holistic approach because that's the healthiest way forward. What does it mean to you to live a balanced life, and what tweaks do you need to make to ensure that whatever you create next will honor your definition of that? As we have discussed, balance is not only a loaded concept in our accepted go-go-go culture but a highly personal measure of how you want to integrate your world. We'll take a clear-eyed look at how to get what we all want.

One of the more challenging concepts to fully embody—and one that I teach with many of my clients—is that you must take responsibility for managing the personal energy you have to expend every single day. You have a finite amount of energy, and spending that wisely, particularly at a time when you are starting to explore and create new realities for your personal and professional lives, will help keep you out of overwhelm and focused on your goals. The concept of energy management is essential to daily performance and healthy self-care, though it's not necessarily sexy. Here, we'll explore essentials like sleep, nutrition, movement, boundaries, communication, and other must-haves that we all know matter but that are easily left on the back burner.

We'll also take a deeper dive into what constitutes meaningful, actionable self-care—and check in with how you're integrating areas of self-care you may not have been considering. Going beyond managing your energy to seriously uplevel your self-care practices is rocket fuel for reinvention. The truth is, we just need more care when we're making changes in our lives. The more nourishment you allow yourself, the more expansive and effective your thinking, creativity, and problem-solving will be. We'll look at practices that even the busiest person can start to experiment with so that you can find a set of simple, custom practices that will fuel and inspire you.

While some of the work of reinventing your reality requires consistent, strategic, and intentional planning and action in the outside world, that goes hand in hand with the inner game of mindset and perspective. Later in this chapter, we'll explore typical stories and beliefs that can trip you up when you're creating change and how to reverse engineer alternatives that will enhance your experience, not detract from it. Part of that work involves cultivating your deeper knowing and desires, so we will wrap up with strategies for unearthing, experimenting with, and indulging your personal interests. They have a lot to teach you on the road to reinvention.

LET'S TALK ABOUT BALANCE

One thing I've noticed throughout my years of doing this work is that "career transition" advice so often leaves out the life part. And "life coaching" often leaves out the work part. Looking at work as a siloed part of your life isn't sustainable, though, and that view results in short-term thinking and decision-making that don't consider the full truth of real life. That is, choosing the work that you are doing in the world is a lifestyle choice as much as a career choice.

In this book, we are operating within that full truth, where the decisions we make about how to use our strengths, values, passions, skillsets, interests, and gifts in the world take our whole lives into account. That means that, yes, we wholeheartedly believe in balance around here. I've written many times about work-life balance on my blog and in my newsletters and been interviewed many times on the topic because I am passionate about debunking the myth that we somehow can't live balanced lives or attain a level of success that is truly sustainable. We must let go of these assumptions for an incredibly important reason: *We will never fully succeed in creating something we believe we cannot have.*

This seemingly innocent and highly practical idea of creating balance in our busy lives has become one of the most fraught topics in modern life. Through our personal and professional communities, we hear all the time the false belief that "work-life balance" is not attainable. We also receive an onslaught of cultural and media messages about what balance is and isn't, along with a host of ridiculous ideas and ideals that are supposed to define for us what it means to have balance in our lives. As a coach, I want to bring a reality check to this nonsense. Achieving a sense of real-world balance in our lives is one of my coaching specialties, and it's one of the most common concerns I hear from professionals who are ready to reinvent a significant area of their life or transition their career. It is certainly possible to not be pulled in so many different directions, to feel a sense of daily peace, purpose, and alignment and live a stress-optional life, and it is possible to feel like you are integrating your life and work in a sustainable way.

Oftentimes, whether you achieve a feeling of balance (or work-life blend or integration, which may be more literal ways to talk about it) does depend in part on how you define that for yourself. Living a balanced life has absolutely nothing to do with slicing life up into perfectly even fractions of a pie. If you have a concept of balance that tells you that each slice of your life will be perfectly divided into equal parts and take up the same amount of time and the same energy, that may well be unrealistic. Few people live that way or find that this approach creates any real sense of balance for them, and why would you want to be tracking and measuring your daily life like that when you are supposed to be living it?

Imagine that you were to create your ideal version of how you spend your time. What are the various areas of life that are meaningful for you right now? Where do you want your time and energy to go, and how would you like that to look? Where are you craving more, and where would you love to dial back? Balance, as it contributes to real-life sustainable success, starts with steps that are simple but often overlooked. Some of those you've already started to uncover in the last two chapters: defining what matters most, knowing what you truly want in your life/your days/your work, and choosing to commit to those things. Responsibilities and priorities *will* ebb and flow, and all of us *will* need to be flexible. There are also realities at play in terms of access that can't be overlooked: Not everyone has equal access to opportunity throughout their life, and some of us are faced with additional challenges through no fault of our own. The bottom line, though, is that just like with "luck," we can't wait around waiting for someone to grant us more balance in our lives. We need to create our own.

Sometimes, all this takes are small schedule or priority tweaks here and there. Sometimes, it's about larger efforts, such as better caring for yourself, practicing evidence-based stress reduction, or delegating your weaknesses so that you can access more natural energy and focus. Often, creating balance requires clear conversations with yourself and others so that you can be both true to yourself and honest with others about what's needed. These small steps, when fully implemented, create space, energy, and time for what matters. In other words, balance. Steps to put those priorities into real-life action might include:

- Practical steps like eating lunch away from your desk, creating an exercise schedule, or setting boundaries around work hours.

- Caring for your physical and mental selves more fully or committing to effective stress management.

- Delegating or re-negotiating tasks you don't want to be doing so that you have more energy and focus (and honoring that you are allowed to delegate and don't need to do everything on your own).

- Assessing the difference between your daily fuel (things like your strengths, favorite tasks, downtime, what gives you energy and uplifts you) and your daily drains (crazy deadlines, poor eating habits, tough commutes, workplace conflicts, conversations you're avoiding). Adding more fuel or reducing drains can be a simple and effective way to calibrate your balance.

Finding a sense of sustainable balance—knowing that you have the mental and physical capacity for the things that matter most to you—does not have to be as difficult as it's often portrayed. It does mean, though, taking ownership and telling a different story about what is within your influence and control. In many cultures, the message has so long been one of pre-deciding that fulfilling, balanced lives are a magical feat of impossibility or an unattainable standard that we've all bought into. Organizations and businesses are run on this belief. And it's a conversation that needs to change. While this skewed narrative may absolve us, collectively and individually, from doing the work to create the thriving that we crave (also collectively and individually), it hasn't made us happy or effective. It's resulted in an epidemic of burnout and a new, stressed-out normal that is literally killing us. High levels of burnout in areas from corporate environments to healthcare to academia were well documented before the 2020 coronavirus pandemic, but the worldwide disruption has taken an even greater toll for many. Today, the statistics are staggering.

So in your reinvention, you will not be leaving balance to chance or, worse, to the whims and expectations of others. You'll bake it in from the start. That requires thoughtful answers to a simple question: What does balance mean to you? Before you move on, take a moment to explore what's not feeling balanced in your life right now. Can you think back to a time when you did feel like you had more balance in your life? What was happening then? What was different? Now think about your future vision. What about this version of "what's next" feels balanced to you? What would it need to include to feel even more balanced, by your definition? What will you design from the start to ensure that you are moving in that direction?

ENERGY: YOUR RENEWABLE RESOURCE

Wouldn't it be great to have a resource well within your reach that can help you meet your challenges, steer yourself out of overwhelm, and intentionally create positive change? A resource that would help you operate in a way that feels energized, naturally balanced, grounded, and able to handle what life throws at you? Well, it turns out you do. We all do, and the way to access it is simple, but it takes repetition and practice: You focus on what you can control and let everything else go. It's time to meet your greatest renewable resource: your personal energy.

Managing your personal energy is one of the most powerful things you can do to create a sustainable, solid foundation for your life and your work. Why? No one is in charge of your energy but you. Let me repeat that. No one is in charge of your energy but you. You decide how often to top it up and whether to drain it. You decide what you spend it on and how you share it. When you're in any kind of transition process, your personal energy requires some extra attention. The inner work you're doing, the experiments you will undertake, the goals you set require emotional, mental, and physical resources from you. You want to be sure your personal energy is continually refilled along the way. When I refer to "personal energy," I'm talking specifically about five areas—all within your control—where you can make small tweaks, consistently over time and achieve significant results:

- Your body.
- Your mind.
- Your spirit.
- Your emotions.
- Your commitments.

Cultivating and managing personal energy has become a core part of how I live, work, and coach for the simple reason that it's free, anyone can do it, and it works. It's also a bit addictive because once you start reaping the results of taking responsibility for your personal energy, you start seeing ways to do it more and more, and you start feeling and seeing the results. For many of us, though (myself included), it takes continual attention to come off life's daily autopilot and trace back your energy or lack thereof to specific daily choices and habits. It's not difficult, but we tend to have our focus elsewhere in the course of our full lives and responsibilities. Chances are, there's something you can think of right now that fuels you up and makes you feel great. Those are the things we're looking to take control of and expand. All you really need to put this revitalization strategy to work is awareness and a few minutes a day. How you do it is a highly individual process. But to get you started, here are a few ideas for energy management practices to experiment with.

NOTICE YOUR ENERGY

What's energizing you, and what's draining you today? How does your body feel? What's on your mind? Take a daily inventory to gather the data you need to make realistic adjustments. Get to know how you operate, and when to boost your energy and when to honor it.

BUILD A PHYSICAL FOUNDATION

This means, yes, the basics of getting good sleep, moving your body several times a week, eating whole foods, and accessing preventative healthcare. Physical energy management doesn't need to be an overhaul of your routine, and right now, I'd suggest that it not be unless health and fitness are the part of your life you're reinventing. Small wins like a healthier breakfast or 30 minutes of daily movement can pay off quickly. I am personally a fan of massage and yoga, two foundational energy practices for me. I have been doing both regularly for the last 18 years. No matter what my schedule or salary (and at times those answers were "busy" and "low"), these two things have been non-negotiables in my calendar and in my budget. Not only does taking care of my body in these two simple ways help manage stress, but it also helps my whole body function more optimally.

PROTECT YOUR MENTAL ENERGY

Whenever possible, find ways to single-task or batch your tasks as much as possible so that you are not mentally switching gears all the time. When you are mindful of what you're focused on and check in from time to time to see if you're putting your attention where you want it to be, you become an observer of your attention. Guard your mental space with regular breaks. One thing that can be especially revitalizing for your energy during times when you're working on what's next is to create stricter boundaries about your media and information consumption or social contacts, focusing specifically on investing your energy on whatever and whoever feels revitalizing and inspiring for you.

CONNECT THE DOTS SO THAT YOU ARE MORE ALIGNED

Instead of operating on autopilot as we so often do, when you practice being more intentional with time and energy, you know exactly what you are getting for what you expend. For example, how does what is on your calendar relate to what you say is important to you? It becomes much easier to connect the dots between what you believe and value and what you do. Sure, it takes time to adjust so that you are living your values through time and energy, and most of us periodically revisit and readjust every now and again. Ultimately, though, this practice can plug huge drains on your energy.

BUILD IN CONSTRUCTIVE REST

I can't stress enough how important this "white space" is during those times when we are exploring, designing, and implementing changes. Slow down and carve out time to relax, physically and mentally. Again, these can be super simple adjustments to make. For example, you might use your commute to unwind with your favorite music or go for an unplugged, mindful walk around the neighborhood. Take a ten-minute time out for a cup of tea. Challenge yourself to a digital detox every week. However feels best to you, ensure there is time on your calendar for moments of renewal and spending restful time with your favorite people.

FEED YOUR SOUL

Finding ways to spend more time doing those things you're great at and that you enjoy doing can unleash pent-up energy we did not even realize was stuck. One easy way to start is to begin identifying the places where you can delegate, drop, or redesign the tasks that drain you, at work and at home. Combine this with carving out even a small bit of time every week to engage in activities that fuel your energy and help you feel a sense of flow, ease, and enjoyment, and you have a winning energy combination. Not sure what fuels you in that way? Put down this book right now and write down ten things you love to do. Now you have your list for the times when you need it.

MANAGE YOUR EMOTIONS

While learning to attune and manage our emotional life is a lifelong practice, it's one we can start to engage in by intentionally building more positive emotions—joy, gratitude, inspiration, awe, love, amusement—into our days by regularly choosing activities and thoughts that cultivate them. Those emotions, in turn, broaden the scope of our attention, thoughts, and actions in a positive way, while negative emotions have the opposite effect. In her research at the Positive Emotions and Psychophysiology Laboratory at the University of North Carolina Chapel Hill, Dr. Barbara Fredrickson refers to this as the broaden-and-build theory. When it comes to the less-than-positive emotions, though, it's also important to feel what you feel and not push it aside in favor of what feels good. All emotions contain information, so allow them to show up and move through you. This also includes recognizing and letting go of emotions that don't belong to you but that come from cultural, community, media, or family messages. When negative emotions arise, there may be a need to set a boundary, have a needed conversation, let go of an old story—whatever that information tells you is necessary to recalibrate yourself.

COMMIT CONSCIOUSLY

The obsession with being busy and living for the hustle and grind is the opposite of strong energy management. It's also a current drug of choice for much of Western culture. As you revitalize yourself so that you can move closer to your vision, I invite you to consider your commitments carefully to ensure you have time and focus for the areas that truly matter to you and the changes you are wanting to create. These questions can help:

What happens if you say yes? What happens if you say no?

Where does this align with your priorities?

How does your body feel about this commitment?

Does saying yes to this help create a bigger, better life?

What do you need right now?

Where can you better manage your energy so that you have the renewable resources you need to be at your best and prepare yourself for the next step toward your vision? As you start to manage your energy more intentionally, I promise it will free up time, mental space, emotional bandwidth, and physical energy to dream more fully and design what's next for you. It will also open up a whole new level of meaningful self-care, which we'll address next.

INTEGRATING NOURISHMENT INTO YOUR REINVENTION PLAN

When I think about the most creative and fruitful times in my life, when I feel most capable of creating what's next in my life, there is one thing that stands out. No matter what else is happening—and in some of those cases, there was a lot happening and much of it not fully within my control—I was prioritizing a deeper level of self-care. I've found the same to be true in my practice. I can be a bit of a stickler around this topic in my coaching because I know firsthand that it's the times when putting your well-being first seems impossible, or at least a tough ask, when it's most critical. It's also when you'll notice the most immediate results. For some of us, and certainly for the external messages we're surrounded with, the idea of self-care conjures up spa days and bubble baths, vacations, beautiful linens, and luxury purchases (or retail therapy). While I personally enjoy some of the trappings that we associate with popular ideas of self-care (I love a good spa day!), that's the tip of a very large iceberg, and it's not what we're talking about here. It's also a narrow and often female-focused view of what it means to take care of ourselves, and in my experience, everyone needs to implement this vital practice equally.

So when I reference self-care, I want to be clear about what I mean by that term. In fact, it feels like such an overused or misused concept that over the years, I've decided to rename it. To me, it is all about nourishment on four distinct levels of being—mind, body, spirit, and environment. Usually, we know where in our lives we're feeling nourished and where we need to increase our supports, boundaries, pleasures, and comforts. Right now, take a moment to do a quick inventory. When you think about these four areas of your being, what feels most nourished and nourishing for you in your current reality? Where are the deficits? Can you identify areas where you need to bring in more of what you enjoy, where you may need to set firmer boundaries about what is negatively impacting or distracting you, or where you just want to feel more supported?

Usually, places will immediately spring to mind as ripe for a little upgrading—that's where you want to focus your revitalization efforts. Those are the places where you'll feel impact quickly and start a chain reaction of upgrading the levels of nourishment throughout your life. If you need a little boost to your thinking around this topic, here are a few places you can start to take a look at.

What tiny change could you make to a daily routine that would make it feel nourishing?

What part of your home or office environment could use a comfort or pleasure upgrade?

What have you been doing to cultivate your spiritual life, personal growth, or sense of awe at something larger than yourself?

Who are the people you love to spend time with but don't connect with as much as you would like? Who are the people you need to have a tough conversation with that has been weighing on you?

When was the last time that you had bodywork, saw your doctor, or took care of routine medical appointments?

Where are you practicing financial self-care, and where not?

What kindness have you extended to friends or family recently that you could extend to yourself, too?

What's one thing you want that you've put off allowing yourself, convincing yourself that you don't really need it?

What's one thing you could do that would remove a stressor or an irritant from your daily life?

What's one tangible item or service that would make your life easier in some way?

I want you to think expansively about this. Yes, whatever you focus on should feel good because nourishment is the end result, but it also may feel challenging because you're no longer skimming the surface of what will nourish you. I'm asking you to stretch here. Doing this inquiry and putting additional nourishment into place in your life may feel uncomfortable at first. It's not always easy to replace simple comforts with what you want more, develop stronger boundaries, and make decisions that feel truly revitalizing, but with practice, it will start to become a habit. Now that we've made self-care a key part of your Reinvention Plan, let's explore other areas of belief that will create a solid foundation for what's next.

WHAT GOT YOU HERE WON'T GET YOU THERE

Maybe you have heard this long-repeated mantra, which is often mentioned when we think about behavior changes that may be required to make significant leaps in our lives or take on bigger goals. Essentially, it means that if you keep doing the same thing, you're going to get the same result. But before we design those changes, we need to shed the old beliefs that created those behaviors, choices, and decisions (and the identities we have built around them) in the first place. In many cases, there's nothing wrong with what got you here, to your present with all that you have accomplished and experienced. But to change course and invent something new, you also have to bring new beliefs to the table so that you can become the person who is able to do those new things.

Coaches spend a lot of time working with beliefs, and honestly, we can often overcomplicate it. One practical way to think about beliefs is that they're the stories we've created by thinking similar thoughts over time. As we repeat these stories, they become familiar, and we can start to lose the perceived separation between what we think and who we are. This happens to all of us, and it's a completely natural function of the brain. Fortunately, thanks to the process of neuroplasticity, those stories can be rewired with new evidence and patterns. With enough practice, we can offer new evidence to our brains, and our neural pathways learn to respond differently. We can change the stories we tell by repeatedly telling a new one instead. We put a lot of weight on our beliefs because our brains are wired to perform that way.

As you redesign your life, you're inviting in more uncertainty. You're asking yourself to stretch and do things you may never have done before. Even when that feels exciting and fresh, even when you've been thinking about the changes for some time, and even when the time is perfectly right to make a move, the more primitive parts of your brain will get kicked into gear. Expect it and make allowances for this. It's a normal response. What feels like resistance, stuckness, or a hesitancy to make decisions and take actions that you know will move you forward is often just the brain doing its job to ward off potential threats. The more you're prepared for this reality, the less mind drama you'll get caught up in along the way. In my experience, knowing what is happening on this neural level can be tremendously helpful. It allows you to recognize it and not be caught off guard, which creates more ease. It also creates space to examine the beliefs you currently hold about yourself and the area you're looking to change so that you can weed out the ones that may be getting in the way.

To be fair, this takes intention, repetition, and time. From a practical standpoint, this type of mindset work isn't simply "positive thinking," "manifesting," or "believe it and it will come." It's more a matter of "practice believing it, and you are more likely to act in ways that will change your results." What kinds of mindset work are most helpful for reinventing your reality and revitalizing your life and work? Clearing mental space and conscious awareness of what you're thinking.

Clearing mental space is essentially decluttering your busy mind. There are many ways to do this, but a few evidence-based practices to start experimenting with include meditation, journaling, focused physical movement such as running or yoga, established healthy routines that allow your mind to settle, breathwork, and quiet prayer or contemplation. Dropping down into the present moment can create a more focused awareness of yourself and your surroundings. These activities allow you to identify and access the choices that influence behavior, bringing awareness to the moments where you move from thought to action. They also open the door to more creative thinking and clearer access to intuition and inner knowing. All of this is incredibly helpful because it brings you right back to yourself and your own circle of influence—that which you can control.

As you clear your mind, you're able to better observe the thoughts that are arising throughout your day. We think 6,200 thoughts every single day, according to recent fMRI research by Canadian psychologists at Queens College—and not all of those thoughts are helpful when embarking on new adventures. Incorporating a focused mindset practice helps identify which parts of your thinking will support you and which may hold you back or limit you in some way. These are the thoughts you want to gently walk away from so that you can take on board more helpful, hopeful, and productive thoughts and let those guide you forward.

Rewriting your limiting or unhelpful beliefs is deep work. You can and will start redesigning your life and creating what's next before you ever tackle all—or even most—of your unsupportive beliefs. In fact, this twofold mindful process will always continue to uncover more stories, beliefs, and narratives you might want to revise over time. What you're doing here is beginning where you are, identifying what is most in the way (or could get in the way), and finding a new, more affirmative, and helpful story you can call on when you need it. Generally, with most people I work with, where to start becomes abundantly clear, and the path forms when you start consciously examining and choosing where you want to spend your thinking energy.

LET YOUR INTERESTS LEAD

One concern that often comes up during times of reinvention is the desire for a roadmap. We're all looking, it seems, for the answers to our biggest questions somewhere out there—questions like *What needs to change here?* and *What do I really want for my life?* But the answers are never going to be sitting out there waiting for you to find them. They're not hidden in this book, in the next book you read or the next coach you hire, or the next job you take. That kind of thinking instead leads us from the frying pan into the fire. It's what makes you boot up the laptop after a tough week at work and start applying to jobs you're not sure you even want or blindly following "programs" that promise seven steps to lifelong happiness, quick weight loss, a thriving six-figure business, dream jobs and relationships, and other perceived holy grails.

There is a different approach, and it's a lot simpler and less stressful. It will, over time, lead you back into yourself, which is where any solid reinvention needs to be based. Simply follow your interests. The problem comes when you're struggling in a wrong-fit career, trying to put out fires in your life, burned out, or feeling burdened by the weight of your responsibilities—and you don't have a clear sense of where your interests even are anymore. Or when you've relegated what interests you to the "maybe someday," "wish I had time for," or "when I get to" categories of your life. Connecting with your interests, whether that's longtime hobbies or inklings that something sounds interesting to you, is a key component to revitalizing for several reasons. It connects you to yourself, to that still voice inside that is often drowned out. It stretches your courage muscles because it pushes you to trust your own instincts and yearnings. And it gives you an excellent place to begin.

So let's rescue your interests and put them front and center. Reflecting on the work you've done in previous chapters, you may have already resurfaced an old interest or recognized interests you haven't explored or pursued. We're going to reach back, bring them along, and give them real space in your daily life. Here are three practical ways to get started with exploring what really interests and intrigues you.

GET THEM OUT OF YOUR HEAD

First, write a list of the interests that are already surfacing as you read this; include everything that comes to mind: old hobbies, work you wish you were still engaged in, work you have now, fields of study you loved but didn't pursue, paths you've wondered about but haven't taken, jobs that intrigue you, dreams and ideas you've had that piqued your curiosity, topics of books and media you read often. If it interests you, write it down. You aren't going to design every one of these things into your life, so don't hold back.

IDENTIFY NEW INTERESTS

Now, let's push it a little further. What do you yearn for that isn't in your reality at the moment? Who sparks envy or jealousy in you, and why? (There's always something to this.) What feels like it could be really fun to try but doesn't fit your life right now or that just isn't you? What images repeatedly catch your attention? What keeps showing up in your world that you're not engaging with? Add these to your list.

MINDFUL OBSERVING

Spend a few minutes each day for the next week noticing what captures your interest. As you notice, keep adding to your list. Each week after, make a point to explore something on your list. Google an idea you had or take a book out of the library to learn more. Make plans to go somewhere that interests you. Search a job board to see which roles pique your curiosity and make you want to know more. Talk with friends about your new interest or find a social media group to explore. Consistently spend time getting in touch with what interests you—and letting it lead you. The more you do this, the more you build trust in yourself, your instincts, and your ability to identify the paths that make the most sense for your life. This is an invaluable skill as you go through the rest of the reinvention process and begin sourcing more of your direction from inside you instead of out there. Allow your unexplored interests to lead you into more meaning, joy, and fulfillment in your life and your work.

REINVENTION REMINDERS

- A strong and vital foundation is an important building block to sustainable change. You're aiming for thriving over surviving, and that means investing time in healthy and positive practices, boundaries, and mindsets.

- A balanced life is far from unattainable. It's a commitment to defining and committing to what you want most and letting go of the noise. Like most goals worth working towards, it necessitates showing up for yourself in a new way.

- Taking responsibility for how you manage your finite personal energy and how you care for your body, mind, spirit, and set up supportive environments is a non-negotiable part of reinvention.

- Change is a growth opportunity. Prepare for the highs and lows and put practices in place to help you navigate them.

- The topics that fascinate you, trigger your curiosity, or keep you engaged for hours are a clear path to knowing and trusting yourself. Indulge them liberally as you start to redesign what's next for you.

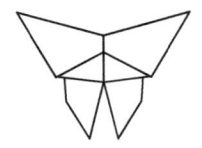

YOUR NEXT STEP

- What does it mean to you to lead a balanced life? If you were to define for yourself how to achieve your vision in a way that feels like "thriving," what would that look like? What would you be doing and not doing?

- Imagine that you can design your ideal schedule based on the commitments that are most important to you. What pieces can you put into place right now to increase your energy and vitality for the work ahead? You can start as small as necessary—tiny moves can yield big results!

- What belief do you need to put in place to support you in the changes you most want to make? Spend a few minutes drilling this down to the actual thoughts behind that belief until you find one that feels true and authentic to you. Create a way to keep this thought front and center for the times when you'll need to call on it.

- Before you move forward, take the time to do a self-care inventory. Which areas will you shore up to nourish yourself and fuel your reinvention?

Ready to dig in? Let's start making it real.

CHAPTER SIX
REDESIGN

LET'S MAKE IT REAL

In the last chapters, you've reconnected to who and where you are currently, identified where you want to go, and created a new vision for the bigger picture of your life. You've also assessed the reserves that you need to sustainably manage your energy, vitality, and mindset for your reinvention journey. If that wasn't inspiring for you and if you feel that your plans, once enacted, won't fully energize you or start you down the path to something that does, I want you to go back and revisit those chapters.

Your vision should be exciting and motivating enough to pull you forward, even if you don't know how you will get there. Your plans should also allow you to feel at your best as much as possible along the way so that you can bring enthusiasm and creative energy to what's ahead. Now, you have a couple of important questions to consider.

> *When you think about what you most want to create next for your life, what specific changes and growth will that require you to make and undergo?*

How can you identify and take steps toward your bigger vision that feel natural, authentic, and doable, not like an uphill climb?

This is the essence of making it real, which is what you will start to tackle as you begin to design a plan that is inspired by your vision, fueled by your vitality, and informed by your personal experience. First, you need a starting point with a measurable and meaningful impact. It doesn't need to be a big shift to begin with, though if you want it to be, that's great. Even the smallest sustainable change in the right area can produce lasting ripple effects out into all other areas of your life, your work, and your well-being. Narrowing down now doesn't mean that you're forsaking all of the other changes and goals you want for yourself. It's actually the opposite. It means you will focus your energy and curate your life around that choice in a way that naturally produces serious forward movement.

In this chapter, we'll also explore what the goals you want to pursue need from you. No matter where you start, there are things you will need to learn and unlearn. You'll uncover habits, narratives, and identities that support you and those that serve as roadblocks. With focus and supportive mindset tools, it's time to map out your direction, identify meaningful experiments, and break your goals down into doable actions with clear results. You'll learn how to test and try out your ideas, fill your knowledge gaps with just enough research, and develop a simple personal strategic plan to follow as you start out on your redesigning mission.

At the end of this chapter, you'll have the bones of an action plan that you can implement right away, and hopefully, you'll have been inspired along the way to get those experiments and research rolling.

CHOOSING YOUR STARTING POINT

Once you know where you're headed, it can be tempting to take on all the things at once, but I can tell you from personal experience that this is an excellent way to become overwhelmed by all of the pieces you need to put in place. The saying "you can have it all but not all at once" applies here. Yes, you can redesign your life in any of the ways you've dreamed. Each piece of your vision can be architected into place over time, but to make that happen, you want to focus on what seems most important to address right now. It may still be what you initially thought when you picked up this book, but often, it shifts by the time you've laid the foundation of Chapters 3, 4, and 5. You might find that something different has come to you while you were doing this work and the place to begin has shifted a bit in priority.

For those who have the tendency to tackle ten projects at once, I hear you, and I have been in those shoes. I've also got three words to share: Proceed. With. Caution. When you challenge yourself to take on every part of your life at once, you open the door to overwhelm and to half-assing a lot of important changes rather than sustainably racking up wins and building solid foundations for your life. That doesn't mean that you won't eventually get where you want to go. I know from experience, having decided to move cross-country, start a business, create a new community, volunteer, buy a new home, heal from trauma, and work on wellness goals all at the same time. This approach does make getting there harder and more complicated than it needs to be. That's why I ask all of my clients—and I am asking you right now—to pick *one* area of focus and choose it intentionally. Even when you are faced, as I was, with many changes at once, you can still choose to dial in your focus on designing one area first while maintaining equilibrium in the other areas of your life. Their time will come.

Challenge yourself to start with one thing, something you can tackle right now, and let the other changes unfold from there. Ideally, you'll choose an area of strategic impact so that you can start to feel the results of your efforts right away. This might mean committing to improving the area of your life that feels most out of balance or most urgently in need of attention. It might also mean strategically taking on an area that, when redesigned to move you closer toward your vision, has the potential to eliminate problems or create downstream improvements in other areas of your life. You might find that you can knock out a whole lot of work by making one big shift in an important area of your life or career.

Where you start is less important, though, than your commitment to take on one area at a time. You'll soon find that your plan to redesign this one area of your life starts to influence and impact everything you do in ways that flow naturally and build on one another. True transformational changes help you powerfully attract and design more of the same.

EVALUATE AND DETOX AREAS OF YOUR LIFE

As you inventory the change you want to focus on, what's happening now in that part of your life? What's holding you back from feeling more fulfilled? What are you putting up with or making do with in this area of your life? Be honest about what's going on for you and assess which of those things are in your control. Once you know what's not working, turn your attention to how you'd like it to be instead. What would it mean for you to fully upgrade that area of your life? How would it feel? What would you be experiencing? You'll need to grow into that experience, so think about what it might require of you to get there. Use your visioning and visualization practices from Chapter 4 to envision the outcome that most excites and energizes you.

Your Redesign plan is as much about letting go as it is about creating. This means it's time to let go of the situations, habits, obstacles, self-imposed roadblocks, self-talk, things you've been tolerating, whatever you've identified that is standing between the status quo and that beautiful vision of success, happiness, and fulfillment in this area of your life. For each item you want to let go of, match it with an alternative—an action, habit, attitude, standard, thought, or anything else you can put in place that feels more fully aligned with what you want. Identifying what to let go of opens up space, and you want to ensure that you fill that space with positive alternatives. We don't want gaps or vacuums; we're putting in the building blocks for growth.

SET YOUR PRIORITIES

Now that you have a good sense of how you'd love this area of your life to be, what it will mean for you to upgrade it, and a few building blocks that will help you do that, it's time to prioritize. As we've discussed, trying to take on everything at once can be a recipe for overwhelm, leaving you starting and stopping but not ultimately getting where you want to go, so again, choose your top priorities for how you'd like to redesign this part of your life. Most importantly, be sure to identify at least a few actions you can take right away and a few habits you already have or can easily develop that will support you in taking action.

CURATE YOUR LIFE FOR REINVENTION

In my previous work life, I spent a lot of time around museums, newsrooms, and marketing conferences. One thing they all have in common is the idea of curating, whether it's collections, education, content, or information. Curation pulls a collection of different items together, preserving them, finding themes, telling a story, and sharing that with the rest of the world. What I've found is that this process of curating is also a powerful metaphor for the Redesign stage of reinvention. Curating is how you establish support structures and systems that allow you to focus and make continual progress toward what's next for you. It's also something you're already doing naturally. We're just going to deploy it more strategically.

You are already the "keeper" of your life. You are the subject matter expert on you. Curating is what you're doing every day as you organize and arrange your daily life. You make meaning out of experience. You share pieces of yourself with others and present yourself to the world. If you're already doing this, imagine what can happen when you are more intentional about what you are doing and how that serves your bigger vision. Imagine what happens when you start organizing, editing, sharing, focusing around your dreams, your inner knowing, your values, desires and priorities, your big wild goals, instead of being all over the place, not focusing or continually comparing your life with everyone else's.

WHAT DOES IT LOOK LIKE TO "CURATE" YOUR LIFE?

Curating is essentially practical reinvention from the ground up. It's one of the most useful tools I used to quit a stressful but perfectly fine job and take on a nine-month action plan to hit the reset button on my life. It's also one of the tools I used to create what came next, piece by piece, and identify what comes after that.

You're deciding what to create through a million tiny decisions every day. Curating means owning these decisions and developing solid decision-making criteria so that those decisions move you closer to where you want to go. You're already deciding what the storyline will be by what you believe, what you say, how you look at the situation you're in. Curating means choosing those storylines that best match your vision and enhance your ability to build that vision step by step. When you're thinking like a curator, you start to focus more on the themes of what you desire to create and why. You can see what is missing and what's already here that you can highlight. You don't start out with all the answers, but you use the resources you do have and gather more around you. As you begin to connect one thing, one idea, one action to another, you leverage a powerful tool for designing the changes you want to make. With a natural focal point, you're compiling the conditions you need to put your plan into action and protecting your time, resources, energy, and attention from distractions.

Through the process of curating around your goal, you can find meaningful paths where you might not have seen them before. You're better able to edit and toss out what doesn't fit and understand that there isn't room for everything, and what you allow into your world needs to fit within that vision you have for your life and your work. It has to feel right and make sense to you. Curating is how you learn to pay closer attention to the environment you're creating and continually build an environment around you that brings out the best in you. Through curating, you're developing the mindset and the strategic reassessment to delete what is not working and find ways to add what you need. Where can you bring in additional ideas, support, resources? As the subject matter expert of your life, you're able to be present with what shows up because you gain the confidence to recognize what is aligned with the life and work you're creating and what's not. (And you can always edit later if you change your mind.)

Another benefit of using the curation method within your Redesign plan is that it helps you take excellent care of who you are and what you have. You become a steward for what really matters, as decided by you. This enables you to design more creative action plans and take calculated risks for your vision. Clear alignment between your foundation and your goal makes it easier to leap when leaping matters and to take a time out when you know in your bones that rest will provide the needed energy for what's next.

As you adopt an attitude of curation, you open yourself to new connections, communities, perspectives, and often unexpected resources and synchronicities. We sometimes identify this as coincidence, but the truth is that you're curating your way into your new reality, day by day.

THE POWER OF BUCKETS AND TINY STEPS

In most cases, the end you have in mind and your vision for launching a reinvention will involve substantial moves, experiments, and investigations. There may be knowledge gaps to fill, skills to build, people to connect with for information or support, ideas to explore so that you can rule them in or rule them out. As you start to identify these things, I want you to also break each one down into incremental steps. When I say incremental, I want you to get really small.

For example, let's say your larger goal is to leave your current job and create your own consulting business. What are all of the steps between sitting in your office this Friday and signing your first client? There's no need to put them in order or to even know all of the steps that may be required. At this point, you're brainstorming all that you currently know needs to happen between those two realities. There will always be steps you haven't thought of, so don't worry if you miss anything. You're focused on what you *do know* right now. You're also not getting into the weeds of how you're going to do those things. You simply want to start to create clarity about what's actually involved.

Once you've got that list, you can arrange it into an ordered series of buckets. For example, in the example of the wannabe consultant, it's a good idea to decide on what services you will offer before thinking about branding or spreading the word about your new venture. You might need to do market research ahead of that. Each bucket will encompass plenty of smaller items. List them underneath as they come to you. Now you have a big picture goal, several smaller milestones, and a laundry list of actions. If you're prone to overwhelm or concerned that you're taking on a difficult shift to make, this map will have the opposite effect. Once it's all written down in your journal, in your planner, in a spreadsheet, app, mind map, or wherever and however you want to organize it, your head is clearer and your job becomes simpler. You fine-tune and follow your plan by continually focusing on the next logical and inspired step. Logical because it's the natural next place to focus that will move your plan forward and inspired because if your explorations are not inspiring you, you won't be following through on them for long.

This map that you create is meant to be a rough guide, pointing out highlights of your journey. It's not a complete itinerary, and like all travel, it is subject to change along the way. But it will definitely show you what you need to do, where the gaps are that you need to fill, and where you need more knowledge, skill, connections, and mindset work. Before you put it into action, there's another step that can be your secret weapon to combat resistance, indecision, and overwhelm as you start to put your Redesign into place: breaking your small steps down even further. Think about this in terms of what would be the smallest action you can take that would further your progress.

Behavioral change researcher and the director of the Persuasive Technology Lab at Stanford University, B.J. Fogg, calls this process "tiny habits," and his work has shown over time how effective they are, not just for building the technology that distracts us every day, but for establishing healthy personal habits and building willpower to make positive changes. He suggests breaking actions down to ensure that they are so small and easy that you can't not complete them. What happens as you rack up these tiny wins by starting with things you can and want to do is that you create both the capability and desire to do more.

I use this concept a lot when coaching clients around goal attainment, self-care foundations, and work-life balance. In my practice, we call it the minimum viable dose—as in, what is the smallest amount you could do in this area and see a result. As you find your minimum viable dose and do only that, you'll soon find that the minimum grows and builds on itself. You'll often find that simply getting started with no pressure (because you're always choosing a quick, easy, and desirable action) is enough to start the flow of forward progress. It is, in fact, how I wrote the book that you're holding in your hands, with one tiny action after the other.

I've included resources for putting the power of curation, buckets, and tiny steps to work for you in the *Reinvent Your Reality* companion workbook available on my website. As you do this work, the important thing is to stay inside the bigger inquiry: *What am I redesigning, and what does it require of me?* and to feed yourself possibility. Both of those states hinge on your ability to make the steps from here to there feel doable within your current reality.

CREATE YOUR PLAN OF ATTACK

In life and career coaching, we often use personal strategic plans or life maps to ground our dreams in reality. The vision you created in Chapter 4 sets the agenda, and the map you've now created helps you get there. You'll use everything you've learned so far to inform your Reinvention Plan, focused tightly around the one starting place that you've identified. Your strategies to get from here to there will incorporate what you now know about your values, your strengths, and your vision for what life is going to look and feel like when you've made this change. They will also incorporate the steps you've identified and will help you identify supportive mindsets and structures, clearly identify the gaps you'll need to fill to confidently execute your plan, and the experiments you'll undertake to get there.

Where does your current reinvention project sit within the larger dream of your vision? How will this one area that you're focused on advance the larger picture of your life? Where does it fit in, and why is it important? If these questions reveal that you need to more clearly define or adjust your goals or plan, now's the time to do this before you get too far down the track. This is also the time to get really clear on the "after" that you're working toward. What will your life look like when you've reinvented this one area of your life? Imagine what will be different and visualize the ripple effects of that change throughout your life. Identify your criteria for success and how you'll know that you've succeeded—how will you measure that? Take a few moments to fully enjoy the sensory experience in your mind and savor what it will be like to have achieved your new reality.

Once you're clear on where you are now and what your desired change looks like, let's ground it in your foundation and give you clear and concrete actions to get started with. How will this desired future help you live a more values-aligned life? Tying your goals to specific values gives them weight and importance in your life and allows you to access a deeper and more meaningful motivation to deliver on your plan. Connecting your goal to your personal resources will be part of your strategy for achieving it. To begin, revisit the strengths, skills, and interests you uncovered in Chapter 3. Leveraging all of these resources in your plan will ensure that your Redesign feels fully authentic to you and easier to enact. Be sure to be specific about what accountability you need in place so that you're fully supported.

> *How will you use your natural strengths, skillset, experience, and interests to create what's next for you?*
>
> *What will be important to include in your plan so that you feel inspired to hold yourself accountable for it?*

You can arrange your plan in any way that works for you, using your buckets and tiny actions to identify what needs to happen first, second, and third, and establish the order for your next steps after that. Build it with clear steps that are easy to accomplish and can be checked off when complete, supplemented with tiny actions wherever needed to build and hold you in momentum. In looking at your plan of action, it usually becomes clear where stumbling blocks or obstacles may come up to slow your progress. For each one that comes to mind, you can brainstorm simple strategies for how you might handle it. If you're not sure what might get in your way, spend some time exploring this so that you are prepared for the inevitable challenges along the way. This may include addressing gaps in your knowledge, tapping into your network for assistance, planning for roadblocks, and ensuring that you have any financial resources or cushion needed to get started. Of course, you won't be able to predict everything—that is why you'll be experimenting, checking in, and realigning your plan as you move forward. We'll discuss some key strategies for this in the next chapter.

Every good plan requires celebration, and we'll be talking more about this in Chapter 9. For now, include in your rough guide any rewards or treats you want to honor yourself with after completing your first three steps and a larger celebration for reaching your goal in this area of your life. This plan will be, essentially, the template for testing and trying out your ideas for what's next for you. It's also a tool you can repeatedly use to launch and work through any additional changes you want to make. As you begin to implement, you will be realigning along the way to ensure that what you're building toward is well-grounded in who you are, who you're becoming, and what matters most to you. You can access a sample Reinvention Plan within the Reinvent Your Reality workbook (see page 176 for the link and QR code).

REINVENTION REMINDERS

- True transformational changes in one area of your life naturally spill over and help you powerfully attract and design changes in other areas of your life as well. Where could you make a change that would have noticeable impacts on other areas of your life?

- Curating your life is a powerful tool for focusing, finding meaningful paths where you might not have seen them before, and ensuring that what you allow into your world fits within that vision you have for your life and your work.

- When you know where you want to begin, getting it all out of your head and into a rough map will help you see the facts of what's involved. Use the minimum viable dose philosophy to put you into action and your Redesign plan to get clear on the resources, mindsets, and clear steps you need to reinvent your reality with confidence.

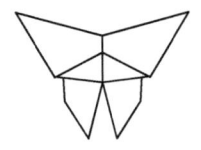

YOUR NEXT STEP

- Get specific and honest about your goal and where it will make the most sense to begin making changes.

  The change I'm starting with is:

  This change is important to me because:

- What do you want and by when? Where do you need to learn, unlearn, access, or grow to get there? Develop a simple but solid plan to get started using the curating and bucket tools in this chapter.

- Identify three things that you could do differently right now to be that person and have that focus. When will you do them? What support do you need?

CHAPTER SEVEN
REALIGN

IT'S TIME FOR A LITTLE REALITY CHECK

It's easy to go off-track with or postpone your goals, dreams, and visions when they're not grounded in the life you live every day. Your environment influences your success, so you want to be sure that yours is working as much as possible for you and not against you. As you test out and implement your ideas, you'll soon have plenty of evidence to help you determine exactly how to fine-tune your plan for sustainable success. In this chapter, you'll focus on that experimentation and research while you continue to realign based on what you're learning by putting your plans into action.

Often the first thing that happens when we start making changes is this: We come up against ourselves. We have the perfect plan, but we don't implement it. We take two steps forward and three steps back. We have minor panic attacks the minute we need to do something that feels unfamiliar. Implementing your plan will mean that you have to step up. Upgrading any part of our life—whether it is your career, your relationship, your financial life, your desire for work-life balance—can bring up any of the doubts, fears, imposter feelings, negative stories you've adopted from the past, and more. In this chapter, you'll explore strategies to deal with them while holding yourself, lovingly, to what you really, really want.

Of course, whenever we're feeling challenged, procrastination can show up, even when that's not our usual way of being. One of the most maligned states of being, procrastination really isn't anything more than information. It's trying to tell you something. In the pages ahead, we'll take a closer look at the message so that you know how to answer its call and not stall your plans. We'll also look at a truth often left out of discussions on reinvention, creating what's next, and generally upgrading your life: It's not always easy, not for anyone. Since we are giving out reality checks here, I'm going to tell you the truth. Yes, there will be hard bits. There will be things you do not want to do, that you regret signing up for, that challenge who you think you are and what you are capable of. Now that you know that, know this: It's not a problem. You can do the hard things.

Part of knowing what you can do—the hard things and the amazing future you are building for yourself step by step—is made easier with proof. How can you know that you can do what you've never done before or reinvent your life to closely resemble the vision that you have for it? What do you do when self-doubt creeps in or you're just having a rough day? You just build the evidence. Finding the evidence for your dream and vision is a fantastic way to stay inspired, motivated, and even open new doors and windows that you never anticipated.

Through it all, you might feel a little resistance. You might feel scared when you test something you need to rethink or when you're stretched a little too far from your comfort zone. Fear isn't to be feared, no matter what Winston Churchill said. It's just a fact of life that you can accept and learn how to use to your advantage with a little practice. Through the practices in this chapter, you'll use these perspective shifts to help you embrace the learning of testing out pieces of your plan and filling the gaps you need to fill. You can realign your plans and enjoy putting them into place, knowing they are grounded, reality tested, and supported by a positive, productive mindset. Your inner game and your outer game will be aligned in working for your success.

WHO DO YOU NEED TO BE TO HAVE THAT?

Reinvention can challenge our personal and professional status quo and deep, core levels of identity and belief. There's nothing like upending things in your life for something new, different, and better to bring up all the beliefs. Beliefs such as *I am alone. I am invisible. Things never really work out for me. I am unloved, unworthy. I need to take a graduate course before I can even think of applying for that job.* And also beliefs such as *I already know that. There's nothing I need to learn here. Everyone disagreed with my plan, so they're all haters.*

These beliefs show up because what we are doing challenges them. We construct these narratives to maintain safety and comfort, and most of the time, they haven't been challenged all that much. But we are more authentic and ultimately safer when we can get curious about why these identity beliefs and thoughts are surfacing and replace them with more powerful identities and thoughts that we are intentionally cultivating. So, how do you do that? To start, it helps to demystify the concept of "beliefs." We think of them as these deeply embedded things, and they can be. But really, if you've ever sat in meditation or even tried to sit quietly without meditating, then you'll know that you have a lot of thoughts. Every second, all day long. Your beliefs are the ones you've practiced, and if you like, you can practice different ones. It will take time for them to catch hold, but they will, and then you will believe something different than you believed before.

Identifying and changing thoughts that are limiting you in some way is a practice of becoming aware of what you're thinking, determining what's productive and what is not, and choosing to keep or replace those thoughts with different ones. New thoughts over time create new narratives. New narratives create new evidence, which creates new actions. While it can often take time, support, and plenty of intentional effort to shift embedded thought patterns, mostly we just need to begin doing it. Actively challenging your thinking is where you start, and this is something we all have experience doing. As humans, our history is filled with beliefs that have been questioned and restructured over time when new evidence, new learning, and new perspectives have come to light. We no longer believe the Earth to be flat or that leeches have a key role in modern medicine. As our cultures have evolved, so have the narratives around what we believe to be true within those cultures. That's what we're calling on here. Think back to something you once believed to be true but that no longer fits what you think today. In some cases, your old beliefs may have fallen away without drama, and in some cases, what you believe today may have evolved through life experiences and intentional work.

As you put your reinvention plans into place, what have you been noticing about your thoughts? Looking at where they are positive, action-inducing thoughts and where obstacle-inducing thoughts are creeping in as well is extraordinarily helpful in realigning your efforts and your plan. What are the beliefs that might be getting in your way? Take out a piece of paper and put a line down the middle. Think about a belief that may be causing you problems. On the left, list the specific thoughts you think when you are believing that. Now, read them to yourself. Notice the emotions that come up when you think that thought. Pay attention to what's happening within your physical body as well. It's probably not feeling great, right?

One by one, challenge those thoughts. In her methodology called The Work, spiritual teacher and author Byron Katie uses a simple question for this process: *Is it absolutely true?* When you examine your thinking, could you easily prove that thought as fact to a judge and jury? For most of us, that is rarely the case, and that's great news because it means that there are plenty of other stories we could tell that could be equally true. On the right side of your paper, write next to each thought another thought that could also be true, one that feels more affirming and helpful, one that brings up better feeling emotions and physical sensations. These are the thoughts to redirect your attention to and where you'll want to expend your thinking energy so that you can gradually rewire your brain to support your desired experience.

When I was in training, one of my early coaching mentors always used to ask me, "*Who do you need to be to have that?*" What I love about this question is that it's real: We all know what it means when we are being ourselves at our best or being our own worst enemy. Thoughts are often at the root of the difference. This thought exercise will very clearly reveal "who you need to be to have that" and what thoughts will help you operate from that place. Who you are being has a huge impact on how your reinvention goes and how it feels along the way. Fortunately, as I learned from that mentor, the first person we need to enlist in getting where we want to go is the only person whose behavior we can control: ourselves!

REALIGNING WHAT GETS YOU STUCK

Have you ever noticed that it usually takes more time and energy to talk about (ruminate about, complain about, think about) doing something than to actually do it? That's procrastination in action, and it's one of the most common blocks that come up when we start to act on our reinvention plans. A former colleague and I have a longstanding private joke about this because it's such a universal experience and one that we were each prone to when we used to work together. Often, when we were on a big project together, we'd encounter delays or tasks we weren't too excited about tackling. While we were really excited about implementing the projects, these tasks weren't getting done. Sure, we could chalk our procrastination up to our busy schedules, our workloads, competing priorities, planetary alignments, what have you—and we did! All of those things can occasionally be valid, and I'm sure our brains could make a defensive case for any of those excuses. But the reality was that it was taking just as long, often longer, to rehash the delays and our negative feelings about doing all the things than it would have to just do the things. When we recognized that this is what we kept doing, we would have a good laugh at ourselves, and one of us would make the point that it was time to get to work. Not surprisingly, our projects took shape pretty quickly every time we shifted the conversation.

Does talking your way around a task, a project, or a step forward instead of moving forward sound familiar? It comes up all the time when realigning. These kinds of delays are likely to happen whenever there's an emotional charge and whenever the outcome is uncertain, and that's most of the time when we're reinventing anything. Maybe it's the thing you dread doing, the thing that's new and scary, or even the thing you most want to do. Knowing what's at play in your emotions and the thought patterns aligned with those feelings dissolves the procrastination block. That awareness alone can help you accomplish many things in half the time. Here are a few reasons you might be staying stuck and mis-channeling your energy and what to do about them so that you can move purposely back into action.

YOU'RE IN A PROCRASTINATION HABIT

It may be as simple as a habit that keeps you circling. If that's the case, chances are you talk a lot about things you're going to do or plan to do or "have to" do before ever actually starting. If this is you (and this was my colleague and me!), consider the time and energy you're expending on planning, talking, or pre-gaming and how that pre-game chatter keeps you in the gap between where you are and where you're headed.

YOU DON'T KNOW HOW TO BEGIN

Sometimes, you really do need more information or need to build knowledge or skill before it makes sense to jump fully into the actions in question. Sometimes, you need a role model, a mentor, or a thinking partner to brainstorm what's needed. Allow yourself to step back and identify specifically what you need so that you can map out the steps to get it. This is usually a lot simpler than we make it out to be, so come back to your stuck place when you're feeling more prepared and see what changes.

YOU WANT TO STAY SAFE

You can't fail if you're not taking on new and scary actions, right? This keeps many people stuck, particularly when their thoughts about failure are that it is wrong, bad, or unacceptable. It's none of those things. It's often a catalyst for growth. When ideas are just ideas, there are few consequences. There are also few results. Talking about that book you're going to write and not writing (something I've been guilty of more than once) or complaining about your unsatisfying job or relationship but not doing anything to improve or leave the situation are surefire ways to feel the illusion of safety. They're also really unsatisfying ways to spend your time and energy because you're holding yourself back from growth and fulfillment, and they will definitely stall out your Reinvention Plan.

YOU WANT TO BE LIKED

When something is important to you—a business idea, a creative project, a career move—it's easy to get caught up in identifying with it. That can paralyze the most motivated among us into inaction. Your idea can't be found lacking if you don't share it and execute on it. Your new promotion won't ruffle any feathers if you don't go for it. Yes, it may be scary, but transformation requires that you let go of wanting to please others and approach your next steps with a greater good in mind, one that includes your own well-being and a fuller level of trust in yourself. It's time to refocus your identity and self-worth back where it belongs: inside you and not attached to external influences and outward goals that leave little time for what is truly going to fuel your forward expansion.

YOU HAVEN'T GOT A SOLID PLAN

A desire to know exactly where you are headed, how you will get there, and what it will look like so that you can have prudent safeguards in place keeps many people stuck and not moving forward. The antidote? Go ahead and make that plan. You cannot be certain how circumstances will unfold, but you can put enough of a plan in place to honor what you need, what is important to you, and what you are responsible for. Build in more detail on how you will approach predictable challenges in case they arise. For some people, the feeling of having done your homework creates a more tolerable space around the uncertainty that is inevitable with change. If this is you, allow yourself to plan in a way that addresses your need for safety in moving forward.

YOU DISLIKE OR FEAR THE NEXT STEP OR A PARTICULAR TASK IT WILL REQUIRE

The longer you talk about the thing instead of doing it, the longer you get to experience that uncomfortable feeling. Just do it, and you might find it's not so bad. At the very least, it's done and with much less energy expended. You might also brainstorm ways to make the dreaded experience a more positive one by reframing how you will approach it and the mindset you bring to it. You might reconnect that step to your larger vision or make it more pleasant by pairing it up with something you do enjoy. Don't forget to set up a celebration or reward at the end if that's motivating for you.

YOU'RE GAINING SOMETHING YOU THINK YOU NEED BY STANDING STILL

Sometimes there's a good reason why you are not moving toward what you think you want, at least according to your brain. This requires a little investigation into how not moving forward may be providing you with another equally compelling benefit. Maybe, like my client Sara, you really enjoy the learning and the exploration that comes before committing to a course of action, and you don't want to leave that behind. Think about how you can build that into how you go forward with your decision. Maybe, like another client, Daniel, you need a longer timeout to regain your equilibrium before plunging into a new career role. After realizing what was really going on, Daniel created a new timeline that worked better for him and allowed him to effectively execute his planned career transition. Maybe, as several of my clients have experienced, there are very real reservations that need to be addressed before you can confidently act. In this case, revisit the criteria you're using to make decisions and see what you find.

What keeps you circling in procrastination? Before shaming yourself for not moving fast enough or decisively enough, take some time to ask where the resistance is coming from and give it what it needs. Then you can steer yourself back into a more inspired and empowered way of taking your next steps.

INVITING IN THE HARD THINGS

If you've come this far into the reinvention process, you'll come up against this truth: You have effectively invited new challenges into your life. It can be easier not to show up for ourselves in this way, yet backing down usually leaves us moving forward and back in fits and starts or feeling the stress of standing still when we *know* we need to do something different. Taking a stand for a life or career that delivers more of what truly matters for you means that the time will come when you need to set new boundaries, raise your standards, have conversations that feel challenging, find your voice, or otherwise act in spite of discomfort. It may mean that you quit the job, make the leap, take the much-needed timeout, or ask for help. You might need to trust you can take on a more challenging role, honor new priorities, and push yourself right out of your comfort zone into a brand-new experience.

That's confronting by design. It's so easy to slip back into what's comfortable and avoid doing or being consistent with doing what you know needs to come next. But it's in these moments where you make that choice to do the hard thing—and all the moments when you stay the path—that you are allowing and building the next stage of your life, your work, and the next iteration of you. As you experiment and put your plan into action, what's your next hard thing? When you've sorted the challenge in front of you and you've decided to take it on, here are several tips to smooth the way so that you don't have to backtrack too much.

KNOW YOUR WHY

It doesn't matter what the hard thing is. If you're not clear on your motivation and if that motivation is not clearly lined up with your values, it will be difficult to stay the course. As a longtime mentor of mine once advised me when I was trying to decide about what to take on next: Do not commit to anything you already know is not a priority for you. Talk about hard things! He also suggested enacting this rule, which has served me well every time I stretch out of my comfort zone: Don't commit yourself with an agenda. In other words, don't do something you don't really want to do because you think it may help you in some other way. So much drama and struggle lie down these twin paths. When we say yes to these things, they are essentially keeping us away from the true yeses in our life. There are plenty of hard things to do in this life. Choose the ones that actually matter to you. Choose the ones that excite you and skip the ones that are simply a means to an end.

FIND THE FOCUS THAT WILL MOVE YOU FORWARD

For the majority of us, that means intentionally cultivating focus and inspiration. This is a daily job, and as much as we can lean on others, we eventually need to own it for ourselves. It means believing and reminding yourself that you *can* do this. It means letting go of what is outside your control, continually checking in with yourself, and redirecting your attention to where your actions will have a demonstrated impact. Breaking your focus down into weekly and daily routines, mindsets, and actions that will accelerate your progress, the tiniest of tiny habits can help here. Anything that is not moving you forward or filling up your soul will eventually have to go.

TREAT YOURSELF LIKE A TRUSTED FRIEND

If your closest ally, someone you love dearly, was setting out to do something challenging, how would you support them? Instead of setting up a daunting or rigid set of expectations for yourself, consider instead what would really support you best. What types of supports could you put in place now that will help the future you along the way? What would supporting yourself look like? If that level of support feels like a stretch right now, there are places where you can start to put it in place, piece by piece. Providing loving support for your transformational process might feel like a subtle shift, but it comes with significant energetic benefits. Instead of trying to accept the challenge or power through it, try standing in support of yourself the way you would do for someone you love.

DON'T INSIST ON GOING IT ALONE

This is one of the most common stuck places I see with my Reinvention Partnership clients, and I get it. I'm independent-minded, too, and that has sometimes been to a fault. It can feel easier to attempt to lone ranger your challenges as they arise, at least until you have them figured out. In some cases, this can feel like protection, and the brain kicks into gear with all sorts of justifications. If this is you, you can practice allowing in—and seeking out—assistance. Gather your support around you wherever you find it, and design an environment that is filled with reinforcement. Reinvention challenges us to be vulnerable, to not have all the answers, to ask for help. This is an area of growth I've personally worked deeply on and deconstructed and that work has been essential (it's also an ongoing process, like peeling an onion). We do, in truth, go further together.

MAKE IT EASIER BY USING YOUR STRENGTHS

No matter what your unique strengths are, there are always ways to use them to make what's difficult a little easier. This allows you to address challenges in a way that leverages what comes naturally to you, builds your resilience, and gives you the energy to creatively tackle whatever obstacles you face. Leaning into and developing your strengths is a lifelong skill that will continually help you grow, become more self-aware, and flourish. As challenges arise, start the ritual of asking yourself: How could my strengths be helpful in this situation? Where might I be overusing my strengths? (If you're not sure how to identify and develop your strengths, start with the resources in the accompanying workbook and consider hiring a coach.)

ALLOW FOR UNCERTAINTY

When you step out of your comfort zone and into a place of creating something new and different, you don't always know how it will go or how your plans will turn out. This is part of why putting your Redesign into place may, on occasion, feel so daunting or stop you in your tracks. Most of us are deeply uncomfortable with the idea of not knowing or feeling as if we are in control of the outcome, and it turns out that we're hardwired this way. This aversion to the risks associated with uncertainty is in part seated in the amygdala of our brain, and it can take a lot of unlearning and redirection. Understanding what's actually going on helps so that you can plan for it and work around it. Yes, for most of us, it is anxiety-inducing to walk wherever you are unable to fully predict the results, which is most of what you're doing right now. But it can feel a lot worse to know that your desire to control the end result is stopping you from doing what you need to do to get where you really want to be.

GATHER YOUR EVIDENCE

By the time you're testing, trying, and realigning your plan, you're someone who does hard things. If this is not a sentence that you're willing to believe at the moment, then let's take a little trip into your magnificent past. This exercise is so helpful that I often assign it to coaching clients before they undertake anything new or encounter the challenges that come with that. Collecting evidence upfront that you're well equipped to handle inevitable roadblocks shores up confidence and provides good fodder for counteracting the inevitable mind drama that creeps up when we're working with new territory. Here's how it works:

1. *Make a list of every time you've ever done what needed to be done, took a stand for your truth, powered through when you knew it was necessary, made a tough decision, chose the uncomfortable but necessary option.*

2. *For each of these experiences, recall how you did that. What made those choices possible?*

3. *What did you learn along the way that may be useful now? Spend the time to make an airtight case for your ability to meet any challenges you face.*

Without engaging with the hard things, life stands still. When you want to create the next iteration of yourself, personally or professionally, and you want to grow into your vision for what's next, you'll need to expand your capacity to embrace what's new, uncomfortable, uncertain, and difficult internally and out in the world. So here's my coach's challenge to you: As you put your action plans into practice, also practice getting uncomfortable. Find one hard thing that's nudging you today, even if that thing has nothing to do with the progress you are trying to make. Do that thing. As you slowly strengthen those muscles and feel the experience of learning as you go, you will supercharge your tolerance for ambiguity and risk, fortify your ability to realign plans as needed, and flex your way into the future that you've imagined.

STACKING YOUR EVIDENCE

As you put your Redesign plans into action, it becomes increasingly important to be vigilant about where you are expending your time and energy. Unfortunately, it's easy to spend both in ways that aren't necessarily serving what you're trying to accomplish, especially when navigating your way through new possibilities. For most of us, that level of conscious energy management takes a little more intention and a lot more practice.

For example, as we've discussed, you can use the same amount of time to work toward something or to resist doing that work. You can put your energy into cultivating a mindset that will support your goals or getting lost in thoughts that will derail you. The same amount of time passes, whether we're engaged in charting a new course or stuck in a holding pattern. In reality, we humans are excellent at wasting *a lot* of time and energy. I believe this is, in part, because we not only need that meaningful bigger vision to pull us forward, our brains are also looking for the evidence to back it up.

In his book, *Meditations on Intention and Being*, yoga teacher Rolf Gates offers the idea that our world is filled with examples for what we want to create if we look to the world with that frame. This is a key to realigning ourselves on the path to creating more of what we want. He writes:

"My ideal has been made out of the lives of ordinary women and men. I am inspired by the heart-stopping manner in which each of us has the potential to turn an ordinary moment into an extraordinary one, an ordinary action, into something of lasting beauty. I am inspired by moments in people's lives and by skills and habits that play out over their entire lifetimes. I consider whatever success I meet with on a given day due in part to the way others have taught me to live by their example."

I've long had a practice of looking for those examples and developed a coaching tool to help my clients do the same. I call it "stacking up the evidence." Like Gates, my clients and I have found plenty of inspiration in real people doing real things out there in the real world. Whatever you want to create, experience, or be, a relevant example likely exists somewhere, in some form. You will continually find them whenever and wherever you invest the time to look. As you experiment with the steps that will move you to your desired outcomes and investigate potential paths, I encourage you to look for the evidence. When resistance, doubt, fear, or that really unhelpful inner critic comes calling, this evidence is a potent antidote. Here are a few places you might begin to look:

- Examples of people who trusted in their goal, who worked at it, who succeeded.

- Examples of people who believed they could, so they did.

- Examples that light the way to move forward when you're not sure what to do next.

- Examples of helpful skills, strategies, and habits to make your own.

- Examples of people who said hell yes or hell no.

- Examples of people who not only survived but thrived, when faced with adversity.

- Examples of empowering ways of thinking and resourcefulness.

- Examples of taking the unexpected path and succeeding.

- Examples of fulfilling careers, sustainable balance, successful businesses, non-traditional career paths, whatever your vision of your "next chapter" contains.

Chances are very good that someone, somewhere, is out there right now creating or has already created evidence that you can achieve the result you're working toward, too. When you look for these examples and find that they do in fact exist, you now have knowledge you cannot unlearn, knowledge that can serve as an anchor as you start to enact enact changes in your life and realign yourself to what's next for you. As you do your research, you might also find that you need to make some adjustments to your strategy or your end goals. For example:

- You can always make new and different choices than the ones you have been making.

- Your thinking about what's possible, practical, or attainable may need to be challenged.

- The excuses and fears that are telling you "no" have just been unmasked for what they really are: separate from the truth of what you're capable of.

- If these examples become your evidence, they are likely not the only evidence out there. Where else can you look for inspiration?

- What information does your evidence provide that will help you fine-tune your goals?

- What are the strategies, skills, habits, resources, and beliefs that will support you as you move forward?

Small moments and large accomplishments alike can lead you where you want to go, but this evidence can be critical to keeping momentum. As Gates says, we can all turn an ordinary moment into an extraordinary one; you have that ability. You can nourish yourself and leave evidence for those who travel behind you. You can create beauty out of thin air. You can teach and lead by example. You can design a life and a career that excites you. Over and over again, simple everyday choices and big life decisions rely on the evidence you've stacked up to this point. What are your examples? Where are you stacking the evidence? In support of what you most desire to create next, or against it?

Use this tool anytime you find yourself lacking inspiration or struggling with self-belief; go find the evidence. If you're resisting the work, go find the evidence. If you're wondering *how*, go find the evidence. If you need a more empowering mindset, go find the evidence. Pile that evidence high, and if you've been compiling evidence as to why your situation is different and why this would never work for you (that's resistance and we'll be talking about it next), well, then it's definitely time to try stacking evidence on the other side of that argument and see what happens.

BEFRIENDING RESISTANCE

While I've been through the stages of reinvention many times, one thing that has never happened is that I've become fearless. I'm willing to bet you haven't either, and it's not a useful expenditure of your time and energy to try to get there. Why? Because fearlessness, no matter what social media, motivational speakers, and the world out there may tell you, is a myth. It doesn't serve anyone to pretend that life's goal is to crush this vulnerable and human part of ourselves. It's just not. The reality is that you will encounter plenty of fears along the way if your transition is in any way a stretch for you. Since all growth involves some kind of a stretch, we can safely assume that resistance and the fear that is often underneath it will be along for the ride at some point. If we keep in mind that our brains want to keep us safe and comfortable, we can see how reinventing our daily realities is neither of those things because it's challenging the status quo.

You may have heard the adage "feel the fear and do it anyway." I think every coach I've known has said this at some point, and I've probably said it myself. In some ways, it's an empowering philosophy, but I also don't believe it's the whole story. When we accept fear is a natural part of change, that resistance will show up when we start to do things differently, and that these states of being are providing us with solid information we can use for our benefit, we can sort out the "do it anyway" kinds of fears from the "there's something I need to learn here" fears from the "course correct now" kinds of fears.

I did not always believe this. Like many people, my go-to response was always to push my fears out of the way. Many years ago, I sat through a full-day retreat at my local mindfulness meditation center. The topic was fear, and I hoped it would teach me, essentially, how to be fearless. I was sure there was a way to erase that pesky little emotion so that I could get on with the grand visions for my life. I hear this all the time as a coach, too. Think about all the time and energy we waste fighting fear and resistance, and all the drama that follows that moves us no closer to our visions. It holds us back or at least distracts us. Fortunately, a shift in perspective and a lot of practice can make a big difference here; it allows us to choose the meaning we want to assign to this state when we find ourselves in it.

What I learned on that retreat was life changing. It was far more valuable than the idea that I could somehow eradicate fear, "crush it," or at the very least ignore it and speed up the process of getting rid of it. I discovered exactly how fear is a natural, human response to the unknown, and a very useful response, as long as you take the time to understand how it works. That fear I was trying to get rid of was coming up for me for the simple reason that I was tackling a lot of uncharted (for me) territory. Along with practical tips on how to identify, physically interact with, and co-exist with fear, there was something else that stuck with me that day. Perpetuating the mistaken idea that we're supposed to remove fear from our lives can do more harm than good. Fear can be many things—a physically felt sensation, a warning signal, an overdeveloped response to stress, an old friend we're used to relying on. Some of these are more useful than others, but there is nothing wrong with feeling afraid. There is nothing wrong with listening to what scares you and evaluating the truth of it, and there is nothing wrong with admitting aloud that you are not, in reality, without fear. You can work with all of that. Imagine how much would go undone if you waited to feel fearless before you did anything brave in your life? If everyone did?

One of my favorite ways to work with this comes straight from a conversation I had with fellow retreaters at lunch all those years ago: Imagine that managing your fear is like bringing your dog on a road trip. You wouldn't put your dog in the driver's seat because, obviously, you're the one driving the car. Putting your dog in the trunk, muffling its bark, and pretending it's not there would never be an option either. Instead, your dog gets a safe and secure spot where you can see them, and they can see where they are and what's happening. That's how you embrace your healthy, normal fears: You appreciate them for what they are, don't try to ignore or hide them, and don't let them drive. Reinventing anything requires a bit of courage, and courage is all about knowing our fears and our resistance, putting them in an appropriate role, and increasing our capability to act at the same time. That's far more nourishing than trying to eradicate or demonize how we feel, and it's also far more doable. Any time that resistance or fear stops you in your reinvention tracks, try a couple of these realignment strategies:

Be brave elsewhere. Exercise the muscle of courage by trying new things in areas that are less charged for you. Practice standing just on the edge of your comfort zone and acting from that place.

Stop pretending you know the result before it happens. Many of our fears come from our predictions about what could happen, not what is happening right this minute.

Increase your odds. Go acquire whatever knowledge you need to feel more confident and less uncertain within the given situation.

Talk openly about your fear and your decision to act anyway. Enlist friends and supporters to your cause and be honest with them. Vulnerability can be a strength and an incredibly supportive structure.

Instead of demonizing your fears, get to know them better. Like the old Zen story about inviting the monster to tea, what might you learn by inviting your fears in?

Look for the lesson. Maybe you have a fear of failing or not making the right decision. What might that teach you about how you need to move forward right now?

Physically surf the emotion of fear by tracking the physical sensations in your body. Acknowledging the tight neck muscles, sick stomach, or other sensations can help you identify and work with your feelings more effectively. Our bodies are incredibly smart.

REINVENTION REMINDERS

- Procrastination is not an identity. When procrastination sets in, you'll move through it with less drama if you know where it's coming from. Use the ideas on pages 125-128 to track its source.

- Reinventing your reality means a time will come when you need to quit the job or make the leap, ask for help, take on a more challenging role, and honor new priorities. Edge yourself out of your comfort zone into a new experience.

- Obstacles are manageable when you plan for them. What might be in the way of acting in ways that get you what you want? How will you manage around those things?

- Whatever you want to create, experience, or be, an example exists somewhere, in some form. Look for the evidence and keep a tally for when you need to call on it.

- Fear and the resistance that it brings up are natural neurological responses to being in new, unexplored territory—experiment with realigning strategies to handle it and even use it for good.

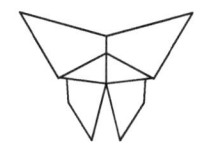

YOUR NEXT STEP

- What have you learned by testing and trying out your plans? What obstacles or redirects came up for you? Identify which strategies you'll use to dissolve the top three obstacles that could derail you from fully enacting and evolving your reinvention plans.

- Add these into your Reinvention Plan.

In the next chapter, we'll explore how you can use what you've learned to fine-tune your plans and get creative about your new personal and professional life because it's here!

CHAPTER EIGHT
RESTRUCTURE

YOU'RE NOT STARTING FROM SCRATCH

As you've come to see throughout this book, none of us ever truly reinvent from scratch. The process is one of adding, subtracting, enhancing, and remixing. There will always be an element of alchemy and creativity in what you're creating. It's current you and not yet you coming together to create the future. Redesigning, testing out plans, and realigning the plan to incorporate what we're learning takes time, but soon the pieces start falling into place and become real. In this part of the reinvention journey, you're well on your way to your destination, and that can feel exhilarating. At the same time, you're standing in new territory with all of the new discoveries that come with that.

In this chapter, we're going to look at some of the typical experiences that happen when your identity is shifting and you are fully immersed in building something new, as well as the mindsets and strategies that will help you make the most of your new reality and surf the waves of identity change and experience that you'll encounter. First, we'll look at why you don't need to have all the answers upfront and how the mindset of exploration can help keep you in motion and help you have fun with whatever comes your way. In some ways, the time when your life is restructuring to make room for what you are creating is a fantastically creative and permissive time. Make the most of it.

In reinvention, we're playing a long game. While synchronicities do happen, and sometimes the universe is perfectly aligned with the right resource or the right connection at the right time, instant results are not really a thing. You'll be building in stages. Every time you upgrade one area of your life, you'll see the ripple effects elsewhere; every piece of your foundation will influence your future results and reveal possibilities you haven't seen yet. Of course, there are always setbacks. You'll probably encounter failures along the way, and that's not only fine, it's great! Expecting failures and normalizing them helps take the sting out of something that might otherwise stop you in your tracks and send you running back to places that may feel more familiar but don't represent what you really want. In this chapter, you'll learn how to handle the times when setbacks arise and why you might want to welcome them when they do.

Finally, we will look at how you're keeping yourself accountable to your goals. Self-accountability strategies are your friend, and they don't need to be complicated. In fact, the simpler and more streamlined, the better.

YOUR REINVENTION EXPLORER MISSION

When we always do what we've always done… nothing will look much different than it looks right now. That's not anybody's idea of successful reinvention, but it happens a lot. Reinventing anything in our lives can be unsettling for one important reason: It requires us to act. When you've done all the groundwork, researched and tested out your ideas, and recalibrated them based on what's come up, the only thing left to do is keep yourself in clear, confident, consistent action. While you want to be sure to employ what you know works well for you, your experience is not always the best path to feeling clear and confident as you start to restructure the parts of your life or work that are in flux. This is the time to stretch. I'm not a fan of the concept of forcing yourself out of your comfort zone altogether. That's just stressful, and it can unleash a cascade of physical and emotional stress responses that, for some people, is more stuck-inducing than motivating.

Instead, let's create an Explorer Mission. My friend Michele and I came up with this term during the period I talked about at the start of this book. I had quit my job, moved cross-country, and given myself six months to experience living in a new city and designing the blend of work-life-business-community that I wanted going forward. I was also keenly ready to have it all in place without the waiting period. One afternoon, I was pouring out my angst about all of the unknowns to Michele, a skilled coach and one of a group of dear friends who I was calling on regularly for support. She reminded me that I had, in fact, willingly chosen to explore a lot of new territories. Maybe I could allow the experience to be new and unknown? Wasn't that the whole point? Of course, that was the whole point. I was on an Explorer Mission, I decided, and that was the lens I used for decision-making for the period of time when I was in that messy middle of figuring things out. The term stuck, and I have refined this idea over years of coaching clients through change. When you're reinventing, it's likely you won't have all the answers as quickly as you might like, especially if you're impatient like me. But you don't need to have all the answers, and in fact, it's better if you don't. You have to test things out. You have to experiment with things you aren't sure will work. You have to do your own homework, research options, and even go down a rabbit hole or two as you decide on what is truly meant for you.

Do I want to explore this? and *What did I learn from this?* have become two of my favorite go-to questions to ask myself whenever I'm in new territory. I hope they'll become favorites of yours, too. With an Explorer Mission, you're off and running. You may get pretty far and feel the exhilaration of everything going according to plan. You'll also fall down or perhaps run into a wall or two. Relax! One wrong turn does not mean it's time to crumple up your plan and toss it in the trash. It means you've learned something and may need to course correct. As long as you are willing to accept that this is all it means, you'll find yourself more and more willing to test and try out your plans, experience it as a living, growing entity, and tweak it accordingly. In other words, don't sabotage your efforts by expecting perfection. Perfection is the most ridiculous idea we humans have come up with yet. In your Explorer Mission, you will treat the idea of "perfect" as science fiction because that's what it is.

As you get deeper into your Restructure, you'll continue the experiments and calibrations you've been doing as you redesign and realign your plans. What I hope for you is that you'll incorporate them as an integral part of your new normal moving forward. That is how you push your edges and stretch into a new reality that is both rooted in what you know to be true and growing increasingly closer to your vision.

BUILDING IN STAGES

As you start to make changes in the one area of your life that you've focused on redesigning, you'll start to notice that many other things start to shift and change as well. That's the natural result of fully upgrading one area of your life; life can't happen in a vacuum. In Western culture, we talk a lot about "getting what we want" and "having it all." It's very passive language. When we take on reinvention, it's an active process that requires us to show up in new and different ways. Over the years, I've heard many stories of how even one small change unleashed a whole new world. It's happened to me, too.

That's in part because the first and most difficult step in getting more of what you want is a willingness to step up and create it. As you take action to influence the experience you're having and the results you're getting, and when you're diligently doing that work, those results and experiences compound across all areas of your life. As you start to notice the effects of your efforts, consider these four strategies that will help you invite even more ripples into any part of your life and work that you desire.

THE CLARITY FACTOR

During the time when you're designing and living into what's next, your initial clarity may get muddy. What you want and, more importantly, why you want it and what it looks like in practice may be in flux. All of this will be evolving as you start to put plans into place. Use this opportunity to connect with the part of you that does know specific parts of the larger picture and listen to what that knowing means for other parts of your life, too.

Consider this:

> *Instead of "I don't know," you might ask what you are sure about.*

Instead of "it doesn't matter," you might ask what does matter most.

Instead of vagueness, you might ask yourself to get more specific.

Instead of settling for the bare minimum, you might ask what would be ideal.

THE FLEXIBLE BIG PICTURE

Another way to leverage the changes you're making into other areas is to pay attention to the moments when something you want is right in front of you, knocking on your door. It's easy to become so narrow-focused or attached to details working out in a specific way that you lose sight of the bigger vision. Sometimes, it's the very attachment to those details that prevents us from seeing that it's arrived in a different package or that something else we'd also love to have has shown up while we're busy building another piece of the vision. Stay your course, but don't miss the opportunity to welcome in the new, too.

Consider this:

Do you want that specific promotion, or do you want meaningful work that challenges you and provides a leadership opportunity?

Do you want to start your own business, or do you want to be home to support your family while contributing to the bottom line?

Do you want a house in that particular neighborhood, or do you want a nurturing environment that feels like home and is close to work?

Do you want a version of your life that feels deeply true to you, or are you being distracted by what works for others?

THE TSUNAMI OF POSITIVITY

We know how effective positivity and optimism are and why it's worth cultivating in your reinvention. A glass-half-full mindset improves your longevity and well-being. Really, though, it boils down to something much simpler than all the research: You can choose a thought that will empower you to move forward or choose one that feels defeating and will hold you back. The more you're choosing the empowered mindset, the one that keeps you in flow, the more that thinking spills over into all parts of your life.

Consider this:

Instead of expecting the worst, what if you expected the best possible outcome?

Instead of complaining to friends, what if you asked them to support you in making your vision into reality?

Instead of paying attention to those who tell you why not, what if you focused on the success stories that your evidence has shown you?

Instead of getting bogged down in what's not working, what if you choose to commit to the possibility of your life as your creation?

THE FIVE-MINUTE MOMENTUM

From a philosophical perspective, one of the quickest antidotes to anxiety, stress, and overwhelm is to act. From a purely practical perspective, we've learned that five minutes is plenty of time to take a tiny step forward. As you adopt this method in working your plan, those steps add up. They also start to shift your approach to other areas of your life, making it easier to enact change in other areas without a lot of time and effort.

Consider this:

> *Five minutes of brainstorming with a friend, colleague, or coach can create better results than five minutes of struggling alone with a problem.*

> *Five minutes of groaning about your ever-growing to-do list robs you of completing or delegating a simple but dreaded task.*

> *Five minutes of chopping up vegetables or blending a smoothie just made it easier to nourish your body.*

> *Five minutes of meditation can help reset your focus, clear your mind, and lower your stress hormones.*

> *Five minutes of doing anything consistently builds a habit, starts a project, creates forward movement, and that mindset ripples out over all areas of your life.*

FAILURE IS PART OF THE PROCESS

For most of us, there will come times when our new reality is not working out exactly the way we envisioned, when setbacks throw us off our game, or when the unexpected comes knocking on the door and it's not a welcome visitor. Setbacks and challenges come in all shapes and sizes. I've personally been through plenty of examples of that, and since you're reading this far into this book, I'm sure you have, too. Failures are a part of life, and how we respond can play the largest part in our experience of what comes next.

How do you navigate this in a positive, empowered, and effective way so that you keep building and even failing forward? Let me share a few things that don't work but that most of us do experience at some point. An ability to experience a negative change as a path to new possibilities doesn't come from most advice that well-meaning people dole out when you are going through challenges. It also doesn't come from stuffing down your feelings so that you can "fake it until you make it" or make others feel more comfortable around your discomfort. Affirmations, although a useful tool when you can see the bridge to your new reality, are not always authentic to your experience when your resolve is taking a hit.

In her Stanford University course on creativity and innovation, Professor Tina Seelig has required her students to write "failure resumes," an exercise designed to integrate the idea that failure is not only a normal part of innovation, but it can also be "the spark that jumpstarts creativity." I love this exercise (you might want to try it, too!) because changing our attitudes about the challenges we often label as "failing" is key to igniting or reigniting that spark.

Moving from challenge to opportunity in your mindset and action is a creative and organic process. That's good news because it means you can influence your results by how you respond, and you don't have to deny any part of your experience to get there. A combination of awareness, choice, and practice will transform your setbacks into new possibilities, so let's break that down.

AWARENESS

Awareness starts with honesty about what you're feeling. Acknowledging the many emotions that come with change is a first step, and it doesn't serve you to shortchange yourself in gathering this data. If you follow your feelings right back to your train of thought, you'll find that how you are feeling in any situation has a lot to do with what you are thinking about that situation. Acknowledging how you're truly feeling allows you to track back to thoughts and narratives that you can revisit and potentially reframe. Taking the time to connect these dots puts you back into your own circle of influence about how you're feeling and how you want to feel about the circumstances at hand.

You'll also want to allow space to process the setback. Clarity is hard to find in a cluttered mind. It doesn't matter how you carve out that space; do what works best for you. When setbacks come up, that can be a great time to revisit the mind-clearing practices from Chapter 5 if you haven't been using them. It's also a great time to experiment with new ways of allowing awareness the space to show up for you.

CHOICE

In her research on positive emotion, psychologist Barbara Fredrickson found that choosing activities, experiences, and interactions that elicit positive emotions results in more positivity across our lives. The awe you feel while standing on a mountaintop, the movies that make you laugh, or the warmth of tea with a close friend—seek out those opportunities as much as possible. The more positivity you invite in, the more upbeat and optimistic you feel.

Shifting your perspective is another effective way to transform setbacks into opportunity. There's never one right way to see things. When you tell the story of what's gone wrong and why, and where you are as a result, listen for truth and facts. How do you know what is true here? What other ways might you or someone else view these same events? There might be a lesson hidden (or not so hidden) inside this experience or an opportunity to see it from a different viewpoint. Try on a few potential perspectives. One benefit of doing this work is that it soon becomes clear how much we can get trapped in our own point of view when there are always multiple ways to see and respond to any situation.

Come back and reconnect to your bigger vision. What are the possibilities that you'd like to see open up in your life as a result of the work you've already done? As you make concrete adjustments to your plan, allow yourself to expand your options wider than you might have at the start. Don't set limits or go by what's previously happened for you. Ask: *What is possible for me now, standing here? What am I discovering now about what I really, really want?*

PRACTICE

Experiment with your new ways of being. Find one daily practice that reflects the empowered, inspired version of you and fully embrace and embody that one. Then add another. When you continually find small ways to stand in your new reality, it gets easier and easier to live there. As you say yes more often to what you're creating, notice what possibilities start to emerge.

As you start to build what's next, you may also want to revisit the work you did in the Revitalize stage to further expand how you are nourishing yourself and your new realities. When you're feeling good and feeling like the person who already has the results you want, that feeling creates its own momentum. When you know what nourishes your body, mind, and spirit, and practice those things as much as possible, caring for yourself at a deeper level than you have previously becomes the new normal. Keep adjusting your standards upward. There is always room for more nourishment, and your investment in expanding your well-being will fuel your reinventions.

Connect to what's possible *every day*. The vision you created in Chapter 4 won't be doing much good hidden under a stack of papers or stashed away. Bring it front and center. Write it out and read it regularly. Create a vision board and post it where you'll see it. Find talismans that remind you of what's possible and keep them visible. Create a mantra, a theme song, a playlist. Make a checklist from your vision and start ticking it off. Set a few related goals and put them on your calendar. Just keep going.

As you continue to embrace mistakes and missteps, don't worry if things are not going perfectly or you aren't "doing it right." Perfect is the enemy of forward progress. All that you need is the trust that you already know enough for your next step. Take that one and let the next ones reveal themselves. In reinventing, you must be willing to act imperfectly, explore, fall down, learn something useful, and use the evidence you already have to know that you can get back up and keep going. How else might you put the idea of *awareness , choice, and practice* to work in service of what's now becoming possible for you?

BUILDING YOUR SCAFFOLDING

One of the keys to creating sustainable changes to your life is to craft an environment that will support the shifts and new realities you've already enjoyed and will continue to develop. Some of this happens naturally, as through the Redesign, Realign, and Restructure stages, you start to attract people, resources, and situations that are more in line with where you're going than where you have been. But there's one thing that can accelerate this process, and that's being very intentional about *all* of the environments you are operating within. In doing this, you're creating an incubator for the vision you're holding and continue to fine-tune.

The importance of creating a supportive environment or building in the scaffolding to support you in what you're creating can't be overstated. No matter how committed you are, battling an environment that is not supportive of your goals becomes exhausting and counterproductive. As a result, you have to push harder and rely on less effective strategies such as willpower or external motivators to stay in momentum. Instead, I invite you to build the most supportive scaffolding you possibly can from here on in. How this looks will be as unique as you are, but your goal is to cultivate an environment that holds you up and supports all of your efforts. Fine-tune the environments surrounding you as much as possible so that they are making life easier for you, not throwing obstacles in your path. In most cases, this may mean that you're experimenting, adjusting, and trying out different strategies and decisions until you find the right mix that will work best for you. That mix will most likely change as you go, so start wherever you are. Just start!

Let's think creatively about what kinds of supports would be most effective for you. There are no limits when it comes to the many ways you can build support for yourself and your dreams and visions, and it can be done on any budget or no budget at all. Just like choosing a redesign focus, it can be very effective to start in one area where you know an upgrade would be really helpful. We all know those places, so tackle those first and go from there. If you've been doing the revitalizing work in Chapter 5, you might have noticed that continually upgrading your environments can initiate that upward spiral. That's because it feels good to feel supported, and when you start taking action to create that support, you naturally want more. Here are a few examples of nourishing environmental upgrades that you may want to start with.

ROUTINES AND RITUALS

Adjusting your morning and evening routines to be more intentional is a simple way to gain a feeling of control and structure for your day. Think about how you'd love to bookend your ideal day and start cultivating that experience, piece by piece. This is not an endorsement of adding another ten things to your to-do list for a so-called power morning. Instead, think "purpose-filled" by starting and ending your day in ways that feel meaningful and nourishing for you, regardless of what other people are doing.

Supporting yourself with a higher level of foundational daily self-care practices such as regular exercise or movement, healthy nutrition, medical care, sound sleep, and stress reduction.

Cultivate wisdom and reflective practices (see pages 171-174 for how to cultivate one that feels right for you).

WHAT YOU LET IN

Meaningful books, podcasts, and films can uplift, motivate, inspire, entertain, and generally cultivate positive emotion in your life.

Limit your news or media intake so that being informed is just that, not a drain on your time, psyche, or well-being.

Curate your social media feeds so that they offer fuel for your dreams and goals, meaningful contribution or connection, and do not induce unhealthy comparisons or a scroll shame spiral.

Clear your calendar of unnecessary tasks and commitments draining your time, energy, or vitality so that you have more room for what matters to you.

PHYSICAL ENVIRONMENT

Curate a physical home and office environment that looks and feels energizing, nurturing, streamlined, creative, or however you most want it to feel. When made deliberately and with attention, even tiny changes make a big difference.

Incorporate living plants, green spaces, and views of nature—known for their profound impact on mental and physical well-being—into your daily routine or environment where possible.

Carve out a small space in your home where you can reliably retreat for a moment of quiet me-time when needed (and use it!).

Add energizing, inspiring, or calming background music, playlists, or soundscapes to your home and your workspace.

Clear clutter, deep clean, and simplify the spaces within your home or office. Doing this periodically can really help recalibrate personal energy and create a sense of calm.

RELATIONSHIPS

Prioritize the relationships in your life where you feel valued and seen for who you are and let go of or re-negotiate how you show up for those where you do not.

Cultivate a community with people who have your back, believe in you, and encourage you to be at your best *right now* while you build out your bigger vision.

Set clear boundaries around your time, energy, or commitments wherever you feel called to set them. Often, we know exactly where these boundaries need to be, and it becomes easier to set them with practice.

Have the necessary conversations to establish a personal boundary, solicit help and support, or express your needs, and make the appropriate request.

For strategies and resources to help with these and other ways to cultivate a more supportive environment, revisit Chapter 5 and the exercises in the Reinvent Your Reality workbook. (See page 176 for the link and QR code.)

YOUR ACCOUNTABILITY PLAN

Throughout this book, you've reconnected with your foundations and your current reality, reimagined your future vision, developed a focused plan, and armed yourself with strategies for putting that plan into action, adjusting it as needed, and staying in momentum. You're leaving with plenty of strategies and some clear ideas about what might stop you in your tracks, as well as a few laser tools to zap those obstacles. You know how to troubleshoot procrastination and resistance when what you want feels out of your comfort zone.

And as you start to restructure your daily realities to match where you're headed and put your plans into place, you will also need reinforcements. It's human nature to avoid uncomfortable feelings, and rewiring our brain to work around that takes time, practice, and structures to support you in that work. Getting comfortable with holding your vision of what's next and reinventing your life to align with it is a skill, and one way to hone it is to know how you'll hold yourself accountable. Here, I encourage you to think past your typical accountability methods and get creative in putting together your own unique structures to hold you up. But first, let's put a few easy wins in place, starting with a self-accountability practice and a simple way to enlist community support.

One way to do this is to look back at what has helped you reach past goals. While we are all individual in terms of what motivates us the most, research shows that positive reinforcement (the carrot versus the stick) and acknowledgment (seeing your tangible progress) can be incredibly effective at helping put your new normal into place. And as we've learned, the big picture vision you spent time creating in Chapter 4 can be highly effective in stimulating areas of the brain that will support you in realizing it, so use that vision to inspire you!

Supportive self-accountability structures may look like:

Tracking your progress in a way that feels energizing and positive to you. Whether you do this with an app, a spreadsheet, a visual tracking sheet in your home or office, or some other way, we tend to pay more attention to what we measure. I've shared some of my favorites in the accompanying Reinvent Your Reality workbook. (See page 176 for the link and QR code.)

Post a visual reminder of your vision somewhere where you will see it every day.

Spend time writing in your journal or planner every day about your goals and progress.

Schedule meaningful rewards for reaching your goal well in advance. Be sure to choose something that feels motivating and celebratory for you—a real treat!

Spend what might at first seem like an unreasonable time on meaningful self-care and fine-tuning your mindset—they are the secret sauce to staying accountable to any goal I have ever achieved, and my clients who adopt this practice always come back with positive results.

Imagine yourself in the future, having restructured your life or work and living fully in the new possibility you've been working on. Rearrange a bit of your day to do something right now that the person who already has what you're building would be doing.

You also may want to leverage the power of community in keeping you actively in pursuit of the reinvention you're working to create. While you do want to be sure that you're selective in choosing who you lean on for this type of support, your community can be an important part of your scaffolding and your accountability plan. You might consider:

Enlisting friends or colleagues to check in with you regularly on your goals and your progress.

Announcing your plan to your social media connections and reporting regularly on your progress.

Writing a blog on your reinvention experience and milestones.

Joining an in-person or online group of people who are taking on similar goals or who are one step ahead of you on the path.

Hiring a coach to work with you and serve as a strategist, sounding board, and accountability partner. (This is what I do, so get in touch!)

Identifying any professional support you may need and finding, budgeting for, and hiring those professionals.

Convening your own board of directors or personal mastermind group to call on individually or collectively when you get stuck or need creative counsel. Be sure, though, that anyone you include understands that their role is to support you and offer constructive feedback. You may even get creative and develop a fantasy board of your most resonant role models that you can mentally reflect on when needed.

Reinvention is ultimately about defining success on our own terms and knowing that what's possible for you is always evolving and growing as you do. After you've put at least one self-accountability into practice and one community accountability into practice, choose a few more elements for your accountability plan, ones that are unique to you, your values, strengths, and goals, and to what you already know helps you feel clear, confident, and committed.

When you describe having successfully made the change you're working on to your best friend, what would you say? How will you hold your own feet to the fire as you move forward with your Reinvention Plan? How will you become *the person who?*

REINVENTION REMINDERS

- You never truly reinvent from scratch. There will always be an element of alchemy and creativity. Your identity is shifting and stretching along the way.

- Reinventing is a process of testing things out, implementing ideas that may not work, doing your homework, and researching your options. It's an Explorer Mission.

- Designing is an active, not passive, process. The first step in getting more of what you want is a willingness to step up and create it.

- Moving from challenge to opportunity in your mindset and actions is a creative and organic process. Use awareness, choice, and practice to transform the setbacks and obstacles on your path.

- Get creative in designing your own scaffolding to hold you up as you rebuild and recreate, including at least one self-accountability practice and one way to enlist support from your community.

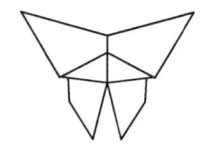

YOUR NEXT STEP

- Identify how you will hold yourself accountable as you set your plan in place. Choose at least two ways. You'll want one for backup.

- Finish this sentence: *I'll know I've succeeded when...*

- In the final chapter, we'll look at what's possible now, how to live reinvention as a lifestyle, and explore creative strategies to keep yourself moving in the direction you most want to go. We'll be sure that you have the support and resources that you need to fully live your life right now while you continue to upgrade your future.

CHAPTER NINE
WHAT'S POSSIBLE NOW

IT'S TIME TO CELEBRATE

Reinvention is a generative and celebratory experience. But sometimes, the high achievers among us tend to speed right through the acknowledgment part of their reinvention journey, headed to their next step. So, I'm going to have you all circle back right now because this doesn't serve anyone. If you believe that you're the kind of person who doesn't need to reward themselves for accomplishing things, then you're exactly the kind of person who needs that most. I know this because I have been that person and I work with them all the time. High achievers, lifelong learners, and high-growth individuals—the kind of people who spend their time doing the thoughtful exercises in this book and working through a clear process to get where they want to go like you're doing right now—can be guilty of not fully owning the small victories along the road to achieving their vision. However, you might have noticed that many of us are happy to beat ourselves with a stick when that victory is slow in coming. Celebrations are the antidote to this as well.

If you've done the work in this book so far and made it through to the final stage of reinvention, then you have plenty to celebrate. It doesn't matter if your celebration is large or small or if you are still in the process with where you ultimately want to go. It's likely that you are. It also doesn't matter how you celebrate, only that you are giving yourself the kind of acknowledgment, reward, or celebration that has meaning and joy for you. You know what you like, you've done the hard work, and it's time to give to yourself in gratitude for a job well done.

From here on in, celebration becomes a regular part of this and any future reinventing you do. Celebrate what's happening in your life, starting here, from this new place you have created for yourself. Treats are important. Not only because they feel good, but because they offer a check-in and a moment to savor your progress and amplify the positive moments. Savoring in itself is a long-lasting treat for your well-being. Research shows that slowing down and savoring the experiences in your life can have profound effects on your well-being and resilience and promotes an optimistic mindset. Slowing down to anticipate, reward, acknowledge, and savor your accomplishments, in essence, creates conditions for thriving in your life.

There's also no better way to create more of what you want than paying attention to how you've already done that. When we take stock of what has worked and what is working, we're adding highly effective tools to our toolbox. Making celebrations a regular part of your new reality will fuel your ability to create more of what you want every day. By seeing reinvention itself as a practice and a lifestyle, as you've been doing throughout this book, you are not continually striving. You are following a natural cycle and intentionally creating what you want for your life and work, living into your vision, piece by piece.

What are you celebrating today? And how will you build celebrations into your plan as you continue to move forward?

Many of us will use this process more than once because we now live in a world where reinventing has become an expected part of life. The skills and strategies you've learned and employed are ones that you'll continue to use and evolve throughout your life. I don't know about you, but a vision of life with few rewards and celebrations sounds pretty dreary to me. So plan those celebrations early and often!

PERFECTING THE PRESENT

From here on in, as you accomplish your plans and live into the reality you've created, it's important not only to celebrate your wins but also to remember to enjoy the journey as you go. While it can be easy to get overly determined to reach your destination (though I encourage you to keep fine-tuning your vision—that's proven to be a powerful motivator!) and fall into striving, that can actually slow down your progress and make you subject to the ups and downs that come with any lasting changes you make.

The way around this is to remember to perfect the present day, the moments you are living in right now, while you build what's next. This philosophy has been driven home to me most often through my hiking activities, as well as my businesses. I recall one day when I was hiking with my husband up a trail that was a lot steeper than I prefer. I love to hike, but the truth is I've never been all that good with steep elevations and I don't enjoy them at all. They're just a part of the process to get where I want to go. On this particular day, we'd unwittingly taken a wrong turn, and as we went higher and higher up the mountain, we came to the slow realization that we were no longer hiking the trail we'd set out on. There would be no viewpoint. No waterfall. Basically, none of the rewards we were expecting. We were lost, and I was already pushing myself a bit more than felt comfortable for me.

At this point, my mind shifted and I could focus on nothing else. Not the beautiful sunshine. Not the fresh smell of the forest around us. Not the lovely ridgeline up ahead. Not the conversation that my partner and I were having. Until, thankfully, he called me on it. Here we were, together in a beautiful place on a beautiful day, having a great discussion about the life we are creating together, and I was so focused on where we were *not*, on what we were *missing*, where we thought we were going that I wasn't even taking in where we actually *were*. I was missing out on things I truly value—nature, companionship, active visioning—all because I was choosing to focus on something else, something that wasn't even real. This was a wake-up call. Typically, I'm one of the most naturally optimistic people I know. I have made it a choice and a practice to notice and appreciate the small stuff. My glass is always at least half-full, and that choice has transformed my daily experience over time. Yet here I was, forgetting something that I deeply knew to be true.

We turned around (realigned) and went a different way so that we didn't end up even more lost. It took me about five minutes to re-tune myself so that I could enjoy the rest of that hike, my day, and the important future-mapping we were doing together. Sometimes, a little reframing is all it takes. It's easy to forget that we can perfect our experience of today while we create tomorrow, and this is never truer than when we believe our stakes are high. But we can do it, and we must. As reinventors, we want to be steadfast in our intention to create the lives and work we desire *while fully living the lives we have right this minute.*

The alternative is that we risk missing so much in our lives, so much that will ultimately inform and enhance any changes we're making and the vision we're working toward. When you don't enjoy the present on the way to the future you desire, you may actually be creating the opposite of what you want because you've abdicated the responsibility to choose your focus. That's what I did while hiking that trail. But like me that day, you do get to choose how you are showing up, even for the hard bits. When you're expending energy on what you do not want, what you think you are missing, what you expected instead of what's here, it's too easy to lose track of experiencing all that is right with this moment and being able to find the gratitude for all that you have before you.

What would change if you embraced your life as it is right now, even in the messy spaces of reinvention? What would be possible if you enjoyed what is while you continue to create the next level? Perfecting the present looks like:

> *Remembering what is within your control and what is not.*
>
> *Cultivating a mindset of supporting your growth, not fixing yourself.*
>
> *Being present for the lesson or the gift in what is true right now.*
>
> *Embracing what's already in place and enjoying it fully.*
>
> *Having more of what you want by tweaking your schedule, your habits, or your actions to have a little of it now.*
>
> *Relaxing into the flow of your evolving life or work.*

Understanding the feeling behind your goals and finding ways to feel that now, not later.

Being aware of all the opportunities that surround you.

Choosing the attitude, energy, and mindset you show up with.

Dropping the idea that your joy and happiness are attached to external circumstances.

Remembering to intentionally make your present as good as it can be as you work on what's next.

LIVING INTO YOUR NEW REALITY

As you continue to build out the vision you've created through this book, you'll experience shifts in how you approach the choices and decisions you're making. I'd like to say that it's all smooth sailing from here, but the reality is that as the owners of human brains and complex lives, it won't always be smooth sailing.

How you stay in momentum and aligned with your new reality will, of course, involve thinking your way through the big decisions. You might make pros and cons lists and enlist your best logic. For many of us, it can be tempting to crowdsource answers from everyone we know (*What would you do?*) and try to outrun doubt by using our best tricks. But I believe the real work is done when we *connect* our way to the answers we're seeking. Confusion about what to do next or a crippling focus on the "how" of our goals and desires is often a disconnection from ourselves, from what we want and from what we know to be true within ourselves.

As you enjoy your new reality and expand the possibilities for where you go from here, it can be helpful to consider creating a regular connection check-in with yourself. This can take the form of evening time with your journal, a regular date with your goal planner, a series of questions that you return to when feeling stuck, an accountability group of like-minded peers, or a number of other rituals or practices that are meaningful to you. How you create this for yourself will be highly individual. What matters is that it becomes a go-to practice you can count on to bring you present and refocus your attention on who you are becoming and what you are creating. To get you started in creating a connection check-in for yourself, here are a few areas you may wish to incorporate.

CORE VALUES

Keeping what truly matters to you front and center is a simple and effective way to ground your decision-making and daily activities. Observe how aligned you are feeling with what you hold most dear and true in your life.

DECISION CRITERIA

Have you outlined specific criteria that need to be met when making important choices about your future? When a decision comes up related to your vision or goals, how will you make it? Having a list of predetermined criteria at the ready can eliminate endless amounts of drama.

A PERSONAL DEFINITION OF SUCCESS

Reinventing your life or work has already required some bravery in setting out what success means to you, not to someone else, to your extended family, your industry, or arbitrary cultural messages. Holding this definition at your center as you continue to create and evolve can often be a big eye-opener. You may want to write it out as a statement for reference.

YOUR BODY

How do you feel in your body when you weigh one choice against another choice? When you think about stretching into a new goal and adding another piece to your long-term vision? Tense? Relaxed? Joyous? Relieved? Nauseous? Walk yourself down your potential paths and watch how your body—the nervous system that is deeply entwined with your brain—responds.

YOUR FUTURE SELF

One of the best mentors and holders of wisdom we will meet in this lifetime is the version of ourselves that embodies who we most want to be. As you work toward what's next, step into what life looks like from that vantage point. Fully see and hear the future you. What are they doing that you could be doing right now? What advice might the ten-years-from-now you give you right now? How would the version of you who has already accomplished this goal handle what you're facing right now?

YOUR VISION

Using your vision as a guiding light can illuminate which potential paths, goals, decisions, and ways of being truly line up with the future as you most want it to be. Whether you have a written vision you review, visualize regularly, or create artwork or visual cues to remind you of where you're headed, check in with it regularly and allow the power of your vision to pull you forward and keep you honest.

YOUR EMOTIONS

How do you feel about what's next for you, what you're building, and any choices facing you? Experiment with taking one or more possibilities off the table and notice how you feel. Becoming familiar with your emotional responses and learning to check in with and discern your rich emotional life can be a wonderfully quick way to realign yourself, better understand your thinking, and tap into your inner truth.

YOUR SPIRIT

What do you know about your future when you're feeling grounded and plugged into your spiritual nature, however you experience that? What does your knowing tell you? For many of us, taking the time to bring this level of centering into our day can have a profound impact on our vitality and keep us more aligned and on track with the future we're building.

Showing up for yourself consistently is where intention and action merge to create new possibilities for your life. As you continue to apply the tools and lessons of this book, you'll always be reinventing, whether it's a small little piece of your life that you're ready to make even more perfect or whether it's a big change that you've now decided to navigate, the tools and lessons in this book combined with a stronger, deeper connection to yourself and your dreams are all you need to keep yourself powerfully moving forward with clarity and confidence. I can't wait to hear what you create.

REINVENTION REMINDERS

- Starting now, your new practice is to celebrate everything. Start by acknowledging the work you've done and any decisions made or milestones reached. Putting into practice a regular practice of acknowledgment for yourself and your wins will in itself open up possibilities you may have never considered.

- You never need to "be done" to reap the benefits of change. We create the future by making the present as fulfilling as possible and showing up to live there.

- Creating a regular practice of connecting to yourself and your vision fuels forward momentum. It also brings you closer to self-awareness, self-confidence, and clarity of purpose. Make your connection check-in a regular fixture in your life.

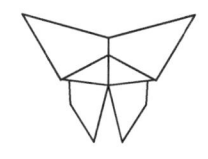

WHAT'S NEXT?

Plan your reinvention celebration. What will you do, have, or experience as a result of going through this process? What do you want to acknowledge yourself for, and how will you do that?

If you haven't already, be sure to download all of the exercises in this book at www.wholelifestrategies.com/ryrworkbook or scan the QR code below.

REFERENCES AND FURTHER READING

Indeed.com for Employers: "Employee Burnout Report: Covid-19's Impact and Strategies to Curb It."
https://www.indeed.com/lead/preventing-employee-burnout-report

Deloitte.com: "Workplace Burnout Survey."
https://www2.deloitte.com/us/en/pages/about-deloitte/articles/burnout-survey.html

FiveTalentsCo.com.au: *Gallup Strengths Development Research.*
http://fivetalentsco.com.au/wp-content/uploads/2018/05/Strengths-Development-Research-Gallup-1.pdf

Clifton, Donald O., *Now, Discover Your Strengths.* Gallup Press, 2001, 2021

Dolev-Amit, T.; Rubin, A.; and Zilcha-Mano, S. "Is Awareness of Strengths Intervention Sufficient to Cultivate Wellbeing and Other Positive Outcomes?" *Journal of Happiness Studies.* 2020.

Wood, A. M.; Linley, P.A.; Malban, J.; Kashdan, T. B.; Hurling, R. "Using personal and psychological strengths leads to increases in well-being over time: A longitudinal study and the development of the strengths use questionnaire." *Personality and Individual Differences.* 2011

Baumeister, Roy F. "Self-Control, High Performance, and the Limits of Willpower." *High-Performance Institute.* https://www.highperformanceinstitute.com/blog/self-control-high-performance-and-the-limits-of-willpower

Neal, D. T.; Wood, W.; and Quinn, J. M. "Habits—A Repeat Performance." *Current Directions in Psychological Science*, 2006.

Young, Sean D., *Stick with It: A Scientifically Proven Process for Changing Your Life-for Good.* Penguin. 2017.

Fogg, B.J., *Tiny Habits.* Mariner Books 2020.

Amabile, Teresa and Kramer, Steven. *The Progress Principle: Using Small Wins to Ignite Joy, Engagement, and Creativity at Work.* Harvard Business Review Press. 2011.

Swarbrick, M. "8 Dimensions of Wellness: A Wellness Approach." *Psychiatric Rehabilitation Journal.* 2006.

Barrett, Lisa Feldman, *Seven and a Half Lessons About the Brain.* Mariner Books. 2020.

Seelig, Tina. *In Genius: A Crash Course on Creativity.* Harper One. 2012.

Boyatzis, Richard E.; Smith, Melvin; Van Oosten, Ellen. *Helping People Change: Coaching with Compassion for Lifelong Learning and Growth.* Harvard Business Review Press. 2019.

Collins, James C. and Perras, Jerry I. "Building Your Company's Vision." *Harvard Business Review.* 1996.

Frederickson, Barbara. *Positivity* - Barbara Frederickson Positivity Ratio

http://www.positivityratio.com

https://peplab.web.unc.edu Positive Emotions and Psychophysiology Laboratory

BigThink.com: Berman, Robby. "New study suggests we have 6,200 thoughts every day." https://bigthink.com/mind-brain/how-many-thoughts-per-day?rebelltitem=4 rebelltitem4

Poppenk, J. and Tseng, J. "Brain meta-state transitions demarcate thoughts across task contexts exposing the mental noise of trait neuroticism." *Nature Communications.* 2020. https://www.nature.com/articles/s41467-020-17255-9

Jose, P. Lim, B.T.; Bryant, F. "Does savoring increase happiness? A daily diary study." *The Journal of Positive Psychology.* 2012.

Stanley, Jan. "The Science of Savoring." Live Happy.com. https://www.livehappy.com/science/science-savoring

Lee, L.O.; James, P.; Zevon, E.S.; Kim, E. S.; Trudel-Fitzgerald, C.; Spiro, A.; Grodstein, F.; and Kubzansky, L.D. "Optimism is associated with Exceptional Longevity in 2 epidemiologic cohorts of men and women." *Proceedings of the National Academy of Sciences (PNAS).* 2019.

Bergland, Christopher. "Optimism Study Gives Optimists More Reason to be Optimistic." *Psychology Today.* https://www.psychologytoday.com/us/blog/the-athletes-way/201908/optimism-study-gives-optimists-more-reason-be-optimistic

ByronKatie.com. "The Work of Byron Katie:" https://thework.com/instruction-the-work-byron-katie/

Nature.com Scientific Reports: "Associations between green/blue spaces and mental health across 18 countries."
https://www.nature.com/articles/s41598-021-87675-0.pdf

Gates, Rolf. *Meditations on Intention and Being.* Anchor. 2015.

GRATITUDE

I don't claim to be the world's foremost expert on reinvention and change. Still, having navigated various forms of personal and professional reinvention throughout my own life and being born with a lifelong love of learning, I have been drawn deeply into the art and science of the why, what, and how it all works. This combination has served me well over many years of coaching others through their own experiences of reinventing their realities to revitalize (and even rebuild) their lives and careers.

Along the way, I developed a passion for sustainable success and discovered that the two are so deeply intertwined as to be one. My reinvention framework is based on this knowing. This book wouldn't have come into being if it weren't for all of the people who contributed to my personal experience, learning, and coaching. It would take a second book to list them all here.

I have daily gratitude for my husband, Michael, who champions and partners with me every day. And big thanks to Michele Woodward for nudging me toward my current profession before I ever knew that was next for me and modeling how to coach with deep integrity.

Thanks most especially to all of the clients in my practice who provide the daily inspiration and personal experiences that further formed my thinking for this book. I appreciate all of the blog readers, draft readers, clients, and editors who helped me refine this framework and the early versions of what you've read here.

And I am so appreciative of the wonderful people who kept it (me) on track, including Lin Eleoff, who rekindled my writing habit, and Lindsey Smith, Andrew Fox, Lucy Giller, and all of their team members who helped bring this book to life. You are all a joy to work with.

And thanks to you for picking up this book and allowing it to revitalize your life and work. I hope it inspires, empowers, and assists you to create more of what you truly want.

ABOUT THE AUTHOR

Sally Anne Carroll is a life and career reinvention coach and the founder of Whole Life Strategies Coaching. As a reinvention strategist and coach, Sally is known as a fierce advocate for designing lifestyles and careers that work together in a balanced, vibrant, and intentional way—and provide more of what matters every day. She is a graduate of Boston University, a professional credentialed coach with the International Coach Federation (ICF), and holds multiple coaching credentials. Her perspectives on career transition, career development, reinvention, and work-life balance have been featured in numerous print and digital media outlets. Sally enjoys a balanced life of her own design with her partner in reinvention and in life, splitting time between Oregon and New Zealand. When not coaching or writing, she can be found out in nature, in her backyard garden, cooking up a new recipe, or planning travel adventures.

Stay connected with Sally, get strategic support for your own reinvention, and share your celebrations and your feedback on this book here:
www.sallyannecarroll.com
www.wholelifestrategies.com

READ MORE FROM SALLY

**Nourish: 28 Daily Dares for Busy People
Craving Sustainable Self-Care**

Let go of old ideas about what's possible, what's practical, and what's necessary when it comes to sustainable self-care. *Nourish* will inspire and challenge you to revitalize your mind, body, soul, and environment with practical, proven strategies that are manageable even on the busiest of schedules. In 28 days, you will:

- Step into powerful, nurturing care for your whole self
- Rewire your thoughts about self-care so that it's foundational instead of trivial, difficult, or time-consuming
- Use science-based strategies to manage your energy, refuel your mind, body, and spirit, and create a more supportive environment around you
- Dial in a personalized self-care foundation you can build on, no matter how busy life gets!

Available at major booksellers and at
www.wholelifestrategies.com/nourish-book.

CPSIA information can be obtained
at www.ICGtesting.com
Printed in the USA
LVHW082109040422
715272LV00003B/98